lonely planet food

EAT VIETNAM

The complete companion to Vietnam's cuisine and food culture

CONTENTS

INTRODUCTION

Many of us are familiar with the cuisine of Vietnam thanks to the Vietnamese diaspora that has settled in towns and cities throughout the world. But nothing compares to exploring the nuances of such vibrant and exciting cooking in the place where it evolved.

As the much-missed globetrotting gourmand Anthony Bourdain remarked of his life-changing trips to Vietnam: 'The food, culture, landscape, and smell; they're all inseparable. It just seemed like another planet; a delicious one that sort of sucked me in and never let me go.'

But how do you start discovering dishes beyond the best phở you'll ever eat in this tall, slim Southeast Asian nation? And with a complex history and a lattice of influences, how do you set out to make the most of your time here without missing an opportunity or making a faux pas? That's where this culinary companion to Vietnam will assist.

Vietnam's capital city, Hanoi, dates back more than 1000 years. Over that time, it has absorbed culinary ideas and techniques from the French, the Chinese and its Asian neighbours. The result is a uniquely intoxicating blend, featuring both noodles and baguettes, that draws diners from around the world. Bourdain was evangelical about Vietnam and in 2016 he and President Barack Obama chatted over $6 bowls of bún chả (see p175) at a street-side restaurant in Hanoi. The bowls of vermicelli noodles, herbs, pork patties and slivers of pork belly, and green papaya all floating in a sweet and sharp broth represent many of the key flavours of Vietnam.

However, to experience everything Vietnam has to offer you have to get out of the capital and into the regions, each of which has its own repertoire of ingredients. This is where English is less widely spoken and where it pays to know how to order food or receive hospitality. In the mountainous north, for example, you can expect a greater variety of rice dishes from the spectacular terraces. However remote a village you reach, the difference in experiencing Vietnamese cuisine in its place of birth is not only down to the fresh and unusual ingredients but more so about your surroundings and how all your senses are engaged with the unforgettable sights, smells and sounds.

HISTORY & CULTURE

© Joshua Resnick / Shutterstock

SO MUCH MORE THAN PHỞ

For many people, Vietnamese food is merely a cheap fill-up: a quick bánh mì sandwich for lunch, a hangover cure via a bowl of phở, or a cold noodle and grilled pork dish with a few spring rolls thrown in. Served up in malls and Chinatowns the world over, from no-frills, family run eateries (often with some pun in the name – 'Phở Real' or 'Phở-King Delicious'), Vietnamese food is often seen as too simple for a special occasion, too 'one note' to eat very often, or too lacking in identity when compared to more popular Chinese, Japanese or even Thai cuisine.

But Vietnamese cooking has finally started to receive some much-deserved recognition, with food personalities such as Anthony Bourdain – who famously dined with President Obama in a Hanoi pork and noodles joint – spreading the word that this Southeast Asian cuisine encompasses much more than simple soups and sandwiches. Vietnamese dishes have made winning entries in TV cooking shows, while celebrity chefs from Vietnamese-Australian Luke Nguyen to Britain's Gordon Ramsay have filmed specials or entire series in Vietnam – and through this exposure, the world has been given a window into a whole new side of Vietnamese cuisine.

Of course, food-adventurous travellers who've been to Vietnam know that what's available overseas is but a tiny tip of the iceberg when it comes to this incredibly diverse cuisine. With three distinct regions and many more provinces, each with its own specialities based on local produce, history and cooking techniques, you could literally eat something different at every meal for a month here – and still have lots left to try.

Vietnam's history of foreign occupation by the Chinese and French, together with its proximity to countries like Cambodia, Thailand and Laos, has added flavour to this complex cuisine. Add in the fresh and healthy nature of Vietnamese food, with its focus on lightly cooked vegetables and accompanying raw herbs and greens, and you have a truly winning combination.

Opposite: Hot, fresh and fortifying, *phở* is the ultimate Vietnamese comfort food

Above: Rice terraces in the hill country of northern Vietnam

Above: Bringing in the day's catch on the south-central coast

THE SOUL OF VIETNAMESE COOKING

While other ingredients may vary, practically every Vietnamese meal will feature the classic mainstays of rice and the ubiquitous fermented fish sauce, *nước mắm.*

In Vietnam, rice is life, both at the table and for the economy. Since the 1990s, Vietnam has been one of the world's top rice exporters, with the production, transport or sale of rice providing an important income stream for the 60 million or so Vietnamese who live in the country's rural and agricultural areas. Rice is so important to the culture that a common way to greet someone is by asking 'Have you eaten rice yet?'

IT'S NOTHING WITHOUT *NƯỚC MẮM*

While rice accompanies every meal, it's really *nước mắm* that defines Vietnamese food. Many other cuisines employ some variation of fish sauce, but *nước mắm* is so central to food here that its use adds a distinctively Vietnamese slant to dishes which share similarities with Chinese, Thai or Korean specialities. *Nước mắm* is used in myriad ways here – to marinate, to preserve meats and vegetables, as a salad dressing or as a general flavouring agent in place of salt or soy sauce (either straight up or as *nước chấm,* a more user-friendly version diluted with water, lime juice and sugar).

A BRIEF HISTORY OF VIETNAM

The massive celebrations for the Millennial Anniversary of Hanoi in 2010 marked a thousand years since emperor Thái Tổ founded Lý Dynasty capital Thang Long (now Hanoi). But Vietnam's history stretches back far longer than this, of course, distinguished by a succession of foreign occupations that have left lasting impressions on the country's culture, religion and cuisine.

Above: Hue, home of the Nguyễn Dynasty's imperial capital

THE ĐÔNG SƠN ERA

Notable periods in Vietnam's early history include the Bronze Age Đông Sơn culture, which emerged in the 3rd century BCE around northern Vietnam's Red River Delta and made huge advances in rice cultivation. The era's best-known legacy are the giant decorated bronze drums which remain an iconic symbol of the Vietnamese people.

From the 1st to 6th centuries CE, southern Vietnam's Mekong Delta was part of the Indianised Cambodian kingdom of Funan. The seafaring Hindu kingdom of Champa ruled parts of coastal Vietnam at around the same time – their sandstone towers still stand around Danang, Nha Trang and Phan Rang, and pockets of their descendants form one of Vietnam's 54 ethnic groups: Hindu Cham on the south-central coast, and the Mekong Delta's Muslim Cham.

© HuyThoai / Getty Images

Left: Thien Mu pagoda in Hue

CHINESE RULE

The Chinese ruled over the Red River Delta for a thousand years from the 2nd century CE, bringing with them dyke and irrigation technology as well as Confucianism, Taoism and Mahayana Buddhism. Ousted in the 10th century, they returned briefly in the 15th century.

TRADERS AND MISSIONARIES

European traders, alongside Japanese and Chinese merchants, began calling at the seaport of Faifo (now Hoi An) in the 16th century, and the arrival of French missionaries in the mid-17th century contributed to the Romanisation of Vietnamese writing, which had used Chinese characters since the 2nd century BCE.

FROM COLONY TO REPUBLIC

In 1802, Gia Long, the first emperor of the Nguyễn Dynasty, unified what is now modern Vietnam from his imperial capital of Hue; but just a few decades later, France annexed Southern Vietnam to their Cochinchina colony. French rule lasted nearly a hundred years, until the First Indochina War and the Geneva Conference led to the forming of the Democratic Republic of Vietnam (North Vietnam) and the State of Vietnam (later the Republic of Vietnam or South Vietnam) in 1954.

After the American War ended in 1975, the country was once again reunited as today's Socialist Republic of Vietnam.

A MIX OF INFLUENCES

Vietnam has been compared to a house with four walls, each with an open window. It's said that while winds may enter the house and rearrange the furniture, the winds that whistle in will always blow out, leaving behind the same table and chairs.

CENTURIES OF CHANGE

With its lengthy borders and long coastlines, Vietnam has long been open (willingly or not) to outside influences, with each new culture adding new ingredients and cooking styles, but leaving behind a cuisine that is uniquely Vietnamese.

Chinese rule gifted the use of chopsticks, noodles, bean curd and stir-frying with oil, while the Mongols – traditional herdsmen who came via China in the 10th century – introduced beef, so laying the foundation for the development of phở, the de facto national dish.

In the south, the proximity of Indianised Cambodia broadened the spectrum of Vietnamese cooking by introducing curries and spices, which the Vietnamese then adjusted to amplify flavour and aroma rather than heat. Thailand and Laos also lent a wide range of flavours, from shrimp paste and chilli peppers to lemongrass, mint and basil.

ENTER THE FRENCH

When the French arrived in the 19th century, they brought with them new techniques like sautéing

Left: Bánh mì, the classic Vietnamese sandwich

Right: Vietnam's cuisine bears a heavy Chinese influence

and baking (and beer-brewing, too), and also shipped in ingredients that reminded them of home: wine, cheese, butter and pâté. And to keep up a year-round taste of home, they planted asparagus, avocados, artichokes and strawberries.

Some foods have survived from the French era with little tinkering, such as the ubiquitous baguettes, stuffed with fried eggs for breakfast or with cold cuts and pickles as an anytime snack. Flan remains a school-dinner favourite, served in little plastic cups, while yoghurt is either eaten in small glass jars or frozen into mini plastic bags and sucked on like a popsicle.

French flavours and techniques have also been co-opted into distinctly Vietnamese dishes like *bò kho*, a rich, full-flavored beef stew with carrots and potatoes that's eaten with a crunchy baguette; or *bánh xèo*, a savoury crepe filled with pork and shrimp. And it's thanks to the legacy of French bakers that inexpensive cream puffs, sponge cakes, croissants and pastries are sold in little shops countrywide – although they may use corn flour, water and oil instead of plain flour, milk and butter.

PLUS ÇA CHANGE...

Given the heavyweight reputation of French gastronomy, it's no surprise that Vietnam's years as a French colony had a significant impact upon the local cuisine. The Gallic influence has even permeated the Vietnamese language – French-derived food-related words include bích quy *(cookies, from the French 'biscuit'),* bơ *(butter, from 'beurre'),* phô mai *(cheese, from 'fromage'), and* ốp la *(fried eggs, a truncated form of 'oeuf au plat').*

BALANCE AND HARMONY

THE CHINESE INFLUENCE

Opposite, clockwise from top: Veggies outnumber chillies in Vietnamese cuisine; spices and and ginger add gentle heat to many local staples

Vietnamese cooking is heavily influenced by China, its massive neighbour to the north and the origin of everyday staples from tofu and noodles to wontons and chopsticks.

SHARED STAPLES

China and Vietnam share the concept of the 'Five Flavours' needed to balance any dish: sweet, sour, salty, bitter and hot (spicy), but with some variations. The Chinese add sourness with rice vinegar and dry cooking wine, but Vietnamese use lime juice, tamarind or pineapple; and here, pungent *nước mắm* trumps salty soy sauce.

Some foods now part of the Vietnamese canon have hardly been altered – Chinese sausages, fried breadsticks, steamed dumplings and sweet tofu pudding – while other dishes have been tweaked to fit the available ingredients and the local climate.

Above: Market-fresh Vietnamese produce

© Todd Brown / Getty Images

© shevtsovy / Getty Images

© Laetitia Lambert / EyeEm / Getty Images

SOME LIKE IT (LESS) HOT

Because Vietnam enjoys warmer temperatures than its northern neighbour, Chinese ingredients meant to warm the body have been substituted or dialled down. In tropical Vietnam, oil and fat are used sparingly, while hardly any dishes achieve the level of spiciness derived from dried chilli and numbing Sichuan peppercorns. Instead, the low-key kick of Vietnamese food comes from ginger, black pepper and cinnamon. Fresh chilli is used, but it's rarely cooked into food. Instead, it's sliced and set on the table as a condiment or incorporated into a dipping sauce.

FRESH PRODUCE

As in China, vegetables play a central role, but they're given a much lighter treatment in Vietnam: instead of being cooked to soft and covered in thick sauces, veg is quickly stir-fried or gently simmered to retain its crispness and colour. And Vietnamese dishes are commonly accompanied by a mound of fresh herbs like basil, coriander and mint with bean sprouts, lettuce leaves and sliced tomato and cucumber.

THE PERFECT BALANCE

The ancient Chinese concept of yin and yang – the goal of striking a balance between opposing forces like hot and cold, invigorating and refreshing – also influences Vietnamese cuisine. This concept explains why the Vietnamese prefer river fish in summer (summer has yang properties, fresh water yin properties), and why certain foods are commonly paired: a sweet and sour soup with salty, caramelised fish; or fish sauce with spicy sliced ginger to go with a grilled, mild-tasting fish.

A LOCAVORE CUISINE

From deltas and plains to coastline, mountains and densely forested highlands, Vietnam's topography is hugely varied. Thanks to this geographical diversity and huge climatic range, Vietnam yields and supports both tropical and temperate crops and livestock – from fish, rice and tea to ducks, beef and coffee.

© Miki Studio / Shutterstock

Above: Fruit delivery in Halong Bay

FISH AND SEAFOOD

Bordered by the Gulf of Tonkin in the north, the South China Sea (East Sea) along the centre and the Gulf of Thailand in the south, Vietnam has nearly 3500km (2175 miles) of coastline and a consequently robust fishing industry. Add to this the endless waterways of the Red River and Mekong deltas and it's no wonder that the average Vietnamese gets through an average of 34kg

A GEOGRAPHICAL ĐÒN GÁNH

Stretching 1650km (1025 miles) from north to south, Vietnam is a long, roughly S-shaped country said to resemble a đòn gánh, the traditional bamboo carrying yoke with rice baskets at either end. The baskets represent the rice-growing regions of the Red River Delta in the north and the Mekong Delta in the south; the bamboo pole is the Truong Son mountains, a long but skinny range along Vietnam's inland western border that's just 50km (31 miles) across at its narrowest point.

(75lb) of seafood per year. In markets and even supermarkets, fish are often alive at the time of sale, deftly killed and cleaned on demand. Excess catches are dried in the sun, then rehydrated in soups or eaten with rice.

REGIONAL VARIATIONS

Outside Hanoi and the fertile Red River Delta lowlands, Vietnam's north is dominated by mountains inhabited by minority ethnic groups who, over centuries, have learned to bend the unforgiving geography to their needs through terraced rice farming, which is supplemented by raising livestock.

Vietnam's central coastal region is better known for seafood production than agriculture. Its lowland areas often experience flooding in the monsoon season, limiting the number of rice crops possible. And to combat the long, cold rainy season here, the cuisine of central Vietnam is often spicier than that in the rest of the country.

South of Ho Chi Minh City and extending to the Gulf of Thailand and the border with Cambodia, the Mekong Delta is known as the nation's 'Rice Bowl'. Fed by tributaries of the Mekong River, the region produces 50% of Vietnam's rice, 80% of its fruit and 60% of its fish. Its proximity to Cambodia also adds a few adaptations of Khmer dishes to the list of local specialities.

© xuanhuongho / Shutterstock

Above: Many regional dishes come with a side of fresh herbs

EATING LOCALLY AND SEASONALLY

Each Vietnamese region has its specialities, from the fresh-tasting treats of the Red River and Mekong deltas to the spiced-up staples of central Vietnam.

RED RIVER DELTA

Bún riêu *Tomato-flavoured broth with shrimp or crab paste and rice noodles.*
Bánh cuốn *Steamed rice-flour sheets wrapped around a filling of pork and wood-ear mushrooms.*
Bún chả *Grilled pork patties and pork-belly slices over rice noodles.*

CENTRAL VIETNAM

Bún bò Huế *Sliced beef and rice noodles in a spicy broth laced with lemongrass, ginger and sate sauce.*
Ớt tương *A spicy paste of minced chillies, oil, sugar, white sesame seeds and garlic, used as a condiment.*
Cá kho *Caramelised stewed fish with fresh chillies.*

MEKONG DELTA

Hủ tiếu Nam Vang *Noodle dish of Khmer and Chinese origin, served with fresh herbs and vegetables and named after Cambodia's capital (Nam Vang in Vietnamese).*
Lẩu mắm *Hot-pot dish flavoured with fermented fish paste, eaten with vegetables unique to the Mekong Delta.*

THE POWER OF FIVE

Many traditional Vietnamese subscribe to the wider Asian belief in the five elements – the fundamental components of wood, fire, earth, metal and water that make up the material world.

THE ELEMENTS AT WORK

These five elements are said to interact with each other, and can create and generate, destroy or weaken: water helps trees grow, nourishing wood, but extinguishing fire; earth produces metal but absorbs water. The 'rock, paper, scissors' children's game originated in Asia as a simple representation of rock (earth) beating scissors (metal), but being overcome by paper (wood).

This concept extends into a wide variety of fields, with each of the five elements having a counterpart in another category, from smells and seasons to actions and animals. As with yin and yang, it's seen as important to strike a harmonious balance between all five elements.

THE ELEMENTS IN PHỞ

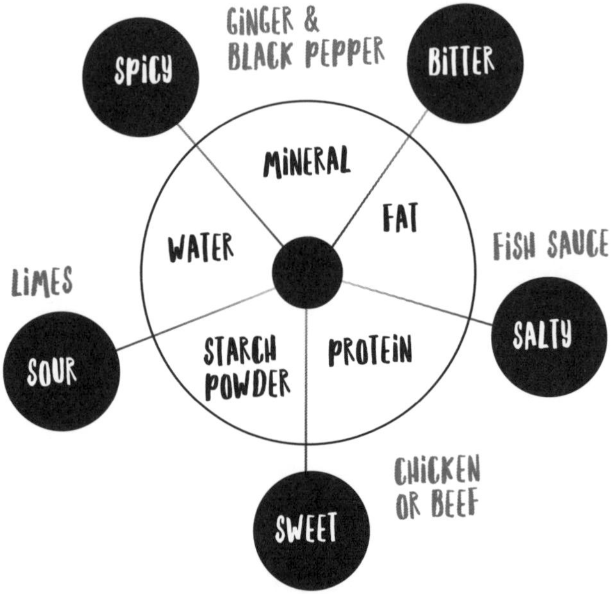

© Elizaveta Galitckaia / Alamy Stock Photo

Above: A five-coloured flag to represent the five essential elements

BALANCE ON A PLATE

Consciously or not, the local belief in the five elements has influenced traditional Vietnamese cuisine. Cooks will attempt to balance each dish among five flavours (spicy, sour, bitter, salty and sweet), include five types of nutrients (powder or starch, water or liquid, minerals, protein and fat), or pair up ingredients that complement each other depending on whether they're hot, warm, neutral, cool or cold.

A bowl of phở achieves this balance perfectly: sweetness and protein from the chicken or beef, spiciness and minerals from ginger and black pepper, sourness from a squeeze of lime, saltiness from the fish sauce. The same could be said about the *nước chấm* dipping sauce that accompanies most Vietnamese meals; a diluted, more user-friendly version of *nước mắm*, it's made with slices of chilli, sour vinegar or lime juice, salty fish sauce, sweet sugar and, sometimes, bitter lime peel.

Vietnamese cooks also try to incorporate five colours into their dishes, a prime example being that ubiquitous Hanoi street food, *bún thang* noodle soup. It's topped with a veritable kaleidoscope of colours: yellow (sliced egg crepe), red (dried shrimp), green (spring onion) and white (steamed pork ham), finished off with a blue/purple dollop of shrimp paste.

THE HUMAN ELEMENT

Within the five elements system, body parts, organs and senses correspond to certain food groups – so the Vietnamese will often drink warm ginger tea against the flu; spots or rashes are indications of too much yin, so mango, beef and garlic ('hot' foods) are avoided. In the same vein, many avoid bitter or spicy foods in summer, and sour in spring.

While the majority of Vietnamese likely won't be able to put the reasoning behind these beliefs into words, they'll instinctively know that some foods should go together – like Vietnamese mint with hột vịt lộn *(fertilised duck foetus still in the shell), or sweet and salty caramelised pork with a bitter melon soup; other pairings just seem wrong for no apparent reason.*

EATING THE VIETNAMESE WAY

Be it a hearty pre-sunrise breakfast before a workday in the fields or a simple dinner shared amongst generations, mealtimes are incredibly important to the Vietnamese and are not to be disturbed – even by the gods.

© Kriangkrai Thitimakorn / Getty Images

Above: Sizzling *bánh xèo*

© John W Banagan / Getty Images

Above: Fresh-baked baguettes

BREAKFAST

In the countryside, breakfast is often served early (between 5.30am and 6am) so that labourers can start work before the day gets too hot. Breakfasts are typically hearty: rice, meat and stir-fried vegetables, or perhaps a bowl of noodle soup with meat and veg.

In the cities, lots of people eat breakfast out, grabbing something light on the way to work – perhaps a baguette stuffed with a fried egg, or a takeaway box of sticky rice and cold meats. Cereal and other instant breakfast foods aren't very popular in Vietnam; most people are far more likely to grab a take-out *phở* if time is short.

IF GOD SHOULD STRIKE, DON'T LET HIM STRIKE DURING A MEAL

VIETNAMESE PROVERB

From left to right: Vietnamese meals are always a shared affair

LUNCH

In the countryside, lunch (and dinner) is the main meal. Workers come home at around 11am for an extended break, with food followed by a nap during the hottest part of the day. A typical lunch might be caramelised pork or fish, cooked with liberal amounts of fish sauce and sugar, and requiring no refrigeration until it's eaten again at dinner. The main dish is usually accompanied by boiled or lightly pan-fried vegetables or a dish of fresh herbs, and finished off with a simple soup of greens in a broth flavoured with dried fish or shrimp. Every meal features rice.

In the cities, lunch spots typically offer *cơm văn phòng*, 'office workers' meals' consisting of small portions of similar courses: a meat dish, stir-fry, soup and rice. Above all, though, mealtimes are social occasions. It's quite unusual to see someone eating alone in a restaurant. Instead, co-workers often have lunch together in groups, be it a team of construction workers or office staff.

DINNER

The evening meal, typically eaten at around 6pm or 7pm, is traditionally when the entire family comes together to eat and socialise. Many rural homes don't have large dining tables, so everything is laid out neatly on the floor with everyone sitting around the food in a circle and sharing dishes communal-style – including a bowl of ever-present fish sauce. In every situation but high-end restaurants and formal occasions, all the food is brought out at the same time, typically on a round metal tray, itself a symbol of community and gathering around to share a meal.

In cities, however, where family members often get home at the end of the school or working day at different times, these traditional dinners may be relegated to just the weekends. Vietnamese typically aren't big on desserts, often forgoing any type of sweets or simply ending on a piece of fresh fruit.

A DASH OF THIS OR THAT

On most Vietnamese tables, condiments will include some fresh sliced chilli, fish sauce (either nước mắm *or the diluted* nước chấm *dipping sauce version), a little dish of salt with sesame seeds or peanuts, some type of pickles (sliced garlic or baby aubergine in the north, leeks or mustard greens in the south), and sometimes a saucer of soy sauce.*

THE HOME KITCHEN

In a country where a separate dining room is a rare thing, the heart of the Vietnamese home is undeniably its kitchen. Far more than just a place where meals are prepared, the kitchen is a place to eat and socialise.

KITCHEN TRADITIONS

In a throwback to the time when wood fires and charcoal braziers meant that cooking took much longer, the kitchen is where Vietnamese tend to gather during the day, from kids doing homework to neighbours popping over to chat while helping to prepare the vegetables. Traditionally, Vietnamese cooks did all the meal prep on the tile floor of the kitchen, from pounding spices with a mortar and pestle to chopping meat and slicing veg. Kitchens had limited space, with room for just basic

Above, from left: Two Vietnamese home kitchens

© Bruno De Hogues / Getty Images; © Adam Young / Getty Images

utensils and a small stock of staples such as sugar, fish sauce, salt, pepper and rice. Until relatively recently, many homes didn't even have a refrigerator either, with cooks making daily or twice-daily trips to the local market instead to buy fresh food.

One essential feature of all Vietnamese homes is the kitchen altar, a simple shrine dedicated to the three 'kitchen gods' who observe everything happening in the home from this central location, and report back yearly to the Jade Emperor just before Tết (Lunar New Year).

RURAL KITCHENS

In the countryside, the typical Vietnamese kitchen will have a back door leading out to a garden, so that the cook can nip out to pick a few fresh herbs and vegetables. Workers returning home from the fields use water from large rainwater-fed urns by the door to wash their feet before entering the home via the kitchen (rather than the front door). Sometimes, country kitchens are located in a separate area towards the back of the home – or even outside, where smoke from cooking fires and charcoal grills can escape.

HAPPY KITCHENS

Kitchens are said to have all the five elements and a balance of yin and yang: metal in the round pots and pans; wood in the chopsticks (one end round, one end square, and evenly matched like husband and wife); water via things like cooking oil and fish sauce; fire in the braziers; and earth in the cook themselves, the centre of the family and the literal and symbolic keeper of the family fire.

KITCHEN KIT

Vietnamese cuisine employs many different cooking methods, and kitchens here are equipped with a few versatile but well-used pieces of kit.

PANS

Shallow pans are used to sauté vegetables, fry fish and cook eggs, while a deeper pan or wok (smaller in diameter and not as deep as the Chinese version) is used for making fried rice and deep-frying spring rolls. A lidded pot is deployed for making soups, usually thin, simple broths flavoured with dried fish or shrimp, or beef or chicken bones, to which a handful of greens and some chopped green onions are added.

CERAMICS

Porous and unglazed, clay pots allow moisture and heat to circulate evenly, sealing in flavours and nutrients. They're usually soaked before use so that the water is released as steam during the cooking process. Slow-cooked clay-pot dishes like caramelised pork or fish are wonderfully intense, with the low-simmered flavours of coconut water, caramelised sugar, garlic, fish sauce and fresh peppercorns all melding together.

STEAMERS

A few homes might also have large steamers, used for cooking meat buns, ham and sticky rice cakes. But without one, a covered pot with a plate, metal rack or even an upturned rice bowl set in a bit of water can be deployed to do the trick.

RICE COOKERS

No Vietnamese kitchen would be complete without a rice cooker. As long as there's access to electricity, even the most modest of homes will likely have an easy-to-use, plug-in rice cooker rather than the traditional pot over an open fire. Still, the Vietnamese tend to ignore the rice cookers' printed lines and use the 'first knuckle' method when measuring out how much water to add to the grains.

TOOLS OF THE TRADE

Vietnamese cooking puts emphasis on fresh ingredients, which tend to require quite a bit of preparation. But as Vietnamese kitchens are typically small, many utensils pull double-duty.

THE BASICS

Most kitchens have several plastic and metal colanders for washing vegetables and herbs; turned over, they double as covers to protect food against flies. Metal-mesh ladles and baskets are also used to blanch noodles and bean sprouts.

In addition to de-skinning veg, peelers are used to shred the fresh banana buds and morning glory stalks that accompany soups, while the knife collection usually includes a cleaver hefty enough to lop the tops off coconuts and cut through bone, as well as a smaller knife for slicing and a shredder to julienne carrots, turnips or green papayas. A sharpening stone is an essential, though mobile knife-sharpening services are easily available.

Other Vietnamese kitchen staples include a mortar and pestle for pounding spices, a pair of extra-long chopsticks for deep-frying, bamboo or metal skewers for grilling, and wooden spatulas for stir-frying.

Above: Vietnamese food prep is a labour of love

© Matt Munro / Lonely Planet

The traditional Vietnamese kitchen doesn't tend to have electric machines like a deep-fryer, meat grinder, hand-mixer, juicer or food processor; most of these tasks are still done by hand. Even manual can openers are relatively rare – most cans have a pull-off top, and for those that don't, a deft jab with a sharp knife usually does the trick. Add rice bowls, soup bowls, small saucers for dipping sauces, table chopsticks and porcelain or metal spoons, and the kitchen is complete.

COOKING METHODS

From a quick flash-fry in a wok to steaming and stewing, Vietnamese cooks deploy a host of different cooking techniques.

SAUTÉING

After adding a bit of oil to a hot pan, the secret of sautéing is to keep the ingredients moving until just cooked. Preparing everything ahead of time is a must, especially by cutting ingredients into evenly sized pieces so that they cook at similar speeds. Meats can be lightly marinated with fish sauce, pepper, sugar and aromatics. Cooks add chopped garlic, shallots and ginger to the oil, and clear a well in the middle of the pan for a dash of oyster sauce or sesame oil to coat the vegetables.

STEAMING

The Vietnamese favour steaming as it's one of the gentlest ways to cook, sealing in the natural sweetness of food and keeping it intact. Seafood, chicken, vegetables and quiches are popular steamed foods. Mild flavours such as beer or a pinch of salt are added to the water, while more pungent ginger, lemongrass and green onions are tossed in with the ingredients.

BOILING

The Vietnamese usually boil meat in cold water, bringing the pot to a rolling boil before adding vegetables. Salt, vinegar or a squeeze of lime are sometimes added to preserve the colour of vegetables; a charred onion or piece of ginger does the same for meats. Being relatively bland, boiled chicken, pork and vegetables are often dipped in some kind of pungent sauce.

GRILLING

Ovens are extremely rare in Vietnam, but grilling over a charcoal brazier (or simply a wood fire) is a time-honoured tradition. The secret to great grilling is to let ingredients sit in a marinade for at least six hours prior to cooking. Typical marinades include sugar, fish sauce, garlic, shallots, lemongrass, chilli and five spice mix; coconut water, honey and untoasted sesame seeds may also be used.

DEEP-FRYING

The Vietnamese particularly like to eat fried foods in winter, from spring rolls and cubes of tofu to battered squid and shrimp coated in flaked young rice. Most supermarkets even carry bags of frozen French fries and

spring rolls, ready for the fryer. The Vietnamese prefer canola or soybean oil for frying – it's inexpensive, low in saturated fat and has a high smoke point.

BRAISING

A small amount of liquid, low heat, a bit of fat and a tightly covered pot are keys to a beautifully coloured, intensely flavoured braised dish like caramelised fish or prawns in their shell. Soy sauce, food colouring, caramelised sugar or even Coca-Cola are used to give Vietnamese braised dishes a rich, dark glaze, and they tend to be salty and sweet – a good budget meal that doesn't spoil easily and can be stretched out with rice.

STEWING

Perfect for fibrous, chewy or hard ingredients such as pigs' feet, lotus root, tougher cuts of beef and dried bamboo, stewing involves cooking over high heat for an extended amount of time to soften and extract flavour. Chicken is sometimes stewed with medicinal herbs and served to pregnant women, those with heart problems or broken bones, and to help people get over a cold or flu.

ROASTED MEAT

Char siu pork and crispy pork belly, or roasted duck, chicken and quail (the latter prized for its golden colour and crispy skin) are stalwarts of Vietnamese cuisine. But given the time-consuming nature of roasting and the special equipment needed, most people buy in roasted meats from speciality shops or roadside grills with a charcoal rotisserie.

Below left: Piles of dragon fruit at a Hanoi market

MARKET MATTERS

Far outnumbering Western-style supermarkets, traditional neighbourhood markets are still Vietnam's preferred place to shop. As a Vietnamese saying goes: 'If you've never been to market, you know nothing. Once you've been to market, you know everything.'

MARKETS V SUPERMARKETS

It's said that you can tell a lot about a Vietnamese neighbourhood by visiting its market – whether it's prosperous or poor, modern or stuck in the past. Larger cities have sprawling markets in multi-level buildings, but the majority of Vietnam's markets – especially in the countryside – are simply a collection of stalls, covered with umbrellas or tarps if not in a permanent structure, and located within walking or bicycling distance of most local homes. These – and the country's ubiquitous sidewalk stalls – typically wind down by late afternoon, leaving only piles of rubbish in their wake.

Whatever form they take, it's hard to imagine Vietnam without the vibrant, soulful markets that showcase each area's personality, whether it be fishing nets and hooks in seaside communities, farming tools and livestock in the countryside,

© Alexander Frais / 500px

Above: Sidewalk stalls offer easy-access shopping on the go

mounds of pickled fish and shrimp in the Mekong Delta or ornately embroidered clothing in the remote markets frequented by minority groups.

But there's a lot to like about modern supermarkets, and they've made significant inroads into everyday life here. Having everything under one roof is a plus, as is the air-conditioning, an attraction in itself for many. But traditional markets – noisy, crowded and unhygienic though they may be – remain alive and well, and are frequented by about 75% of Vietnamese.

THE FRESHNESS FACTOR

One of the main draws of traditional markets is the freshness of the produce. Meat and vegetables are brought in during the wee hours, and savvy shoppers make sure to arrive early to bag the best selection. The Vietnamese like to

FLOATING MARKETS OF THE MEKONG DELTA

Covering some 3000km (1864 miles), the waterways of the Mekong Delta are a lifeline to its people, who have always lived on and near the water. Many make a living from the region's famous floating markets, congregations of barges laden with rice, fresh fruit and veg. Some barges double as liveaboards, and an army of smaller boats zip about selling drinks and meals.

The majority of the trade is wholesale, with smaller boats buying goods to sell on, and the whole scene is as popular with sightseeing travellers as with those here to do business. A four-hour drive from Ho Chi Minh City, Cai Rang is the delta's largest floating market. Arrive early when trading is at its peak and watch the whole scene play out. Go sooner rather than later, however, as floating markets are on the decline, a casualty of cheaper, faster road transport.

© Matt Munro / Lonely Planet

Left: Aerial trading at Cai Rang floating market, Mekong Delta

say that 'fish should be swimming and chickens should be clucking', indicating how fresh they want their products.

Although most homes now have fridges, cooking with the freshest ingredients possible remains the standard. While walking through a market's meat section may be off-putting to some – the sight of freshly butchered meat hanging on hooks and exposed to dirt, dust and flies, and the tiled floors wet with scales and entrails – these are all signs of freshness to those in the know.

You might think that the more expensive meat sold at supermarkets is safer (perhaps it's gone through some type of inspection process?), but it may be somewhat elderly: there's still a lingering distrust of refrigerated meat and a resistance to eating frozen cuts, a non-issue at traditional markets. After all, supermarkets in Vietnam rarely discount meat at the end of the day, while market sellers are eager to sell off butchered meat to prepare for fresh animals the next day.

SENSORY OVERLOAD

Some animals sold at markets – fish, frogs, crabs, chickens and ducks – are displayed alive: stuffed in cages, feet tied together, squirming on trays or swimming in shallow buckets. Buyers pick their protein and the seller offers a death-blow with a well-timed whack to the head for fish or a quick slit of the knife for all the others; de-scaling or de-feathering costs just a bit extra. The smell of fresh blood and wet feathers or the clucking of chickens and ducks crammed tightly under a bamboo basket can be overwhelming, but for the Vietnamese, it's all just a normal part of market life.

THE SOCIAL SELL

Markets have an innately social aspect. It's said that in supermarkets the products have to sell themselves via bold packaging and glitzy promotional signage; but in traditional markets, it's the stallholders who do the selling, keeping regular customers informed about what's freshest and selling at a good price. Most Vietnamese will have a preferred vendor for each type of product, someone they can trust not to overcharge or sell them bruised fruit or old meat. It's a relationship built on trust and familiarity, as stalls are often passed from generation to generation.

EASY ACCESS

Convenience is another major factor in the Vietnamese love of markets. There are no crowded car parks to navigate, big carts to push, or counters where you have to check in bags. Instead, you can drive your motorbike right up to a stall, get what you need and be off in a flash. Lots of products can be bought pre-prepared, too, from minced lemongrass and shallots to salad-ready shredded papaya and banana bud. You can also buy in tiny quantities, from a clove of garlic to cooking oil siphoned into small bags – just enough to make what you need, with no wastage.

But traditional markets do have their drawbacks. They tend to be poorly planned, with goods spilling out into narrow lanes and into the way of traffic and pedestrians. Because they're often located in residential neighbourhoods without any purpose-built infrastructure for water, sewage or garbage collection, they're considered unhygienic and don't mesh with the modern face of Vietnam that the government wants to put forward.

MARKET TIPS & TRICKS

- **WHEN TO GO** *Avoid early mornings if shopping for high priced items. Most sellers are superstitious, believing that their first customer will influence the day's trade – enquiring but not buying is a bad omen. But cold and rainy days are great for shopping, with fewer customers and a better potential for deals.*

- **CHOOSE YOUR SPOT** *Stalls on the edge of a market are more visible, get more traffic and pay consequently higher rents, upping prices to compensate. Head to stalls in the middle of the action for better prices.*

- **A HAPPY EXCHANGE** *Establish a rapport with sellers – a smile or a few words in Vietnamese or simple English go a long way. And if you've had a good experience with a seller, try to go back; repeat customers tend to be valued.*

- **CHOOSE YOUR OWN** *It's tempting to let the seller bag items for you, but if you do, chances are you'll get a few bruised pieces of fruit in with the good.*

- **BARGAIN WITH BALANCE** *Haggling is part of Vietnamese culture – the prevailing wisdom is counter with half the price you're offered; and bear in mind that the more you buy, the better the price. Vendors may up prices for buyers perceived as inexperienced, from solo men to foreigners, but while no-one likes to get ripped off, the amounts involved are relatively small. It's best to approach bargaining as a game – don't get angry, keep smiling, and enjoy the experience.*

Right: Mealtimes in Vietnam are frequently family affairs

EATING ETIQUETTE

Mealtime in Vietnam is a relaxed and upbeat affair. The food is decidedly unfussy, there's no abundance of cutlery, and you can eat as much or as little as you want from the spread of dishes on the table.

MEALTIME MANNERS

The Vietnamese don't have a litany of unspoken mealtime rules designed to trip up the unwary, though you should avoid universally frowned upon practices like chewing with your mouth open, putting elbows on the table or bouncing your leg while eating; other faux pas include using your own spoon to ladle soup from the communal bowl, appearing to dig around the food to find the choicest piece, and using your chopsticks to point. There are also a few general etiquette norms, centred on respecting elders and the communal nature of Vietnamese dining, that you should observe whether in homes or restaurants.

'Respect your elders and take care of the young ones' is a Vietnamese saying that governs mealtime manners. The best seats (closest to the food) and the choicest, most tender pieces of food are reserved for older people, while parents make sure the kids' bowls are always filled. Hosts will also seat invited guests in a position of honour (near the food or opposite the host), and generally make a fuss of them, urging them to eat more and perhaps flipping their chopsticks around to use the non-eating end to put more food in a guest's bowl.

Many families, especially in the country, still sit on the floor to eat with the food placed in the centre. It can be a long way from the floor to your mouth, so it's okay to avoid spillage by holding your rice bowl in your hand, halfway to your mouth. If you need to get up during the meal, definitely avoid walking over the food, even if it means taking the long way around.

As Vietnamese mealtimes are a shared experience, often including multiple generations, the atmosphere should be lighthearted and cheerful, with controversial conversation best left for later. If you finish eating early, carry on chatting until the meal is over for everyone.

© Matt Munro / Lonely Planet

BALANCE AND RESTRAINT

A Vietnamese proverb that's central to mealtimes – 'eat everything and get a spanking; leave food behind and lose your wife' – addresses the importance of not being greedy and eating everything in sight, whilst at the same time avoiding food wastage. During the meal it's also good to 'watch the pot', or keep an eye on how much rice is left. Running out of rice is never a good thing, so if there's only a little left, you should slow down or adjust your rice/main dish ratio. The ideal end to a meal will see some food left on the serving plates (showing the host was generous and the diners weren't too greedy), but nothing left in the individual rice bowls, a sign that the meal was a very good one.

© Peter Stuckings / Getty Images

DURING THE MEAL

Once all the dishes are brought to the table, the host will spoon just the right amount of rice into everyone's bowl. About two-thirds is optimum – not so much that there's no room for the actual food, but not so little that you might ask for multiple refills (considered a sign of greediness). Especially in the north, before anyone starts eating, the youngest in the family will *mời cơm*, voice a short phrase that invites the elders, in descending order, to start eating. It's something like the French 'bon appétit', but more to show deference than to invite someone to enjoy their meal. Once the eldest person begins, everyone else follows suit. If you're a guest, wait for the host to eat first, unless he or she specifically invites you to start the meal.

USING CHOPSTICKS

If you're uncomfortable using chopsticks, it's perfectly acceptable to ask for a fork, either in a home or restaurant setting. Every Vietnamese kitchen will have forks, usually used to eat fruit. However, if you plan on spending any time eating Vietnamese food, it'll do you a world of good to practise your chopstick skills. Rounded and tapered on the eating end and square on the holding end, chopsticks are a veritable multi-tool in the right hands – used for everything from masterfully picking up individual peanuts and mouthfuls of rice to dipping things in sauces, cutting through meat, and holding down a sticky jumble of noodles while someone else takes a small portion.

Start out by making sure your chopsticks are even and that you're holding the right end (the square one). Use your chopsticks to pick up pieces of food, putting them into your own rice bowl first, before bringing them to your mouth. Taking food directly from the serving dish and putting it in your mouth is considered unhygienic.

Vietnamese meals almost always include soup. Quiet slurping is not considered impolite, but making other chewing noises or blowing loudly to cool soup are. It's better to take small spoonfuls from the side of your bowl.

While the Vietnamese typically don't eat with their hands, certain dishes may require it: rolling fresh summer rolls; using a pick to remove the meat from snails; eating boiled crab or grilled shrimp; or wrapping a piece of savoury *bánh xèo* crepe or a spring roll into a lettuce leaf to be dipped in a *nước chấm* dipping sauce.

At the end of a meal, some homes might have a finger bowl filled with weak tea; it's for rinsing hands not drinking. Most homes also have a toothpick dispenser. If the person beside you has finished eating, offer them the toothpicks before taking one for yourself. Always use one hand to cover the mouth if using toothpicks.

© Matt Munro / Lonely Planet

© Mint Images / Getty Images

Above: Serving up the phở
Top right: *Bún bò Huế*

TABLEWARE 101

Vietnamese meals are typically comprised of a main meat dish, stir-fried or boiled vegetables, a soup and rice; there may also be a plate of raw vegetables and herbs, pickles (leeks, mustard greens or bean sprouts) and dipping sauce, either fish (pure or diluted) or soy. Chopsticks and spoons are the only cutlery you'll need: food is cut into bite-sized pieces before cooking, and things like chicken and char siu pork are sliced before arriving at the table. The only exception is fish. If presented whole, the flesh can be picked off using chopsticks. In a restaurant setting, waiters usually apportion out pieces for each diner. Discreetly spitting out fish bones is fine; just place them in your napkin or on the empty plate reserved for bones.

When not eating, rest your chopsticks across your rice bowl, on the edge of a plate or on chopstick rests if available. Soup spoons should rest facing down. Never stand chopsticks upright in your rice bowl, as this carries echoes of the incense burned at funerals.

DIPPING BOWLS

Some homes will have individual dipping bowls, but it's more common to see one communal bowl used by all diners. When dipping food into it, you'll need to be fast and steady-handed so as not to drip sauce in your wake; feel free to hold your rice bowl close to the dipping bowl to minimize open space. Since several people may dip from the same bowl, it's important not to leave bits of food in the sauce, dip anything that's been bitten into or let the tips of your chopsticks touch the sauce.

FESTIVE

While there are dozens of festivals throughout Vietnam, many of them are celebrated only locally, from the monthly Full Moon Lantern Festival in Hoi An to the Bà Chùa Xứ Temple Festival in Chau Doc, near the Cambodian border.

THE FESTIVAL MENU

As well as the countrywide celebrations for Lunar New Year, the Vietnamese also love gathering for special events. Birthdays, housewarmings, weddings and funerals are usually accompanied by a raucous feast, held in homes or under a rented tent on the street out front. The festive foods on the menu are garnished with extra care and are brought to the table in courses, rather than all together like in a regular meal. Dishes may include:

CRAB AND ASPARAGUS SOUP

(súp măng tây)

While asparagus does grow in Vietnam, it's rare to find it in local markets. Combined with hand-picked crab meat, it makes for a hearty yet delicate soupy treat.

STICKY RICE

(xôi gấc)

Thanks to the addition of beta carotene- and lycopene-rich juice from a type of Southeast Asian melon, this glutinous rice takes on a gorgeous orange-reddish hue, making it a favourite at weddings. It's slightly sweet from coconut milk and is a good accompaniment to mild meats like boiled chicken (another festive favourite) and steamed Vietnamese ham.

ROASTED MEATS

Another time-consuming favourite seldom made at home, celebration roasts include chicken or duck, crispy pork belly, suckling pig and pork seasoned with five spice.

FOODS

HOTPOT

(lẩu)

Hot pots are popular during festive occasions due to their quintessentially shareable nature. The table has to work together to add the meat, vegetables, herbs and noodles to the broth, and the time they take to cook is ideal for socialising.

DEEP-FRIED SPRING ROLLS

(nem in the north and chả giò in the south)

Few Vietnamese make spring rolls from scratch due to the number of ingredients (typically minced pork and prawns, mushrooms, glass noodles, eggs and green onions) and the time it takes to roll and fry. But they're popular at feasts, stuffed with crab and mushrooms.

WHOLE FISH

Not many homes have woks or steamers large enough to accommodate a whole fish, so it's a festival favourite, steamed with soy sauce and ginger or deep-fried then topped with a sweet and sour sauce.

FRIED RICE

(cơm chiên Dương Châu)

Filling Yangzhou-style fried rice is often a festive finale – a mix of shrimp, Chinese sausage, Chinese broccoli, barbecued pork, peas, carrots and egg brought out to satisfy anyone still hungry at the end of the feast.

CRISPY SALADS

Popular festive foods because they're extremely colourful, if time-consuming to make, Vietnamese salads of julienned mangoes, lotus stems, banana bud, kohlrabi, heart of palm or green papaya are topped with shrimp, pork or even jellyfish, and dressed in a slightly sweet fish sauce.

DESSERTS

Puddings aren't a huge deal – other than birthday or wedding cakes, typical festive desserts include fresh fruit, flavoured gelatine and individual servings of flan or yoghurt.

TẾT NGUYÊN ĐÁN

There are lots of local festivals and holidays in Vietnam, but the only one that's celebrated nationwide, regardless of religion, ethnicity or location, is Tết Nguyên Đán (Lunar New Year), which falls in late January or early February.

AN AUSPICIOUS NEW DAWN

The arrival of spring is celebrated in several Asian countries, including China, Japan and Korea, but the Vietnamese have their own customs and traditions surrounding Lunar New Year. Many focus on rebirth and renewal (Tết Nguyên Đán translates as 'New Dawn'), as well as rekindling the bonds of family, friends and community.

During the run-up to Tết, Vietnamese families go to great lengths to prepare. A week before, many conduct a ritual to wish the three Kitchen Gods a good journey back to heaven, where they will report everything that happened in the home during the year to the Jade Emperor. The kitchen gets a thorough clean, offerings are placed on the kitchen altar and live carp are bought, to be later released into a river or other body of water – as strong swimmers, carp are said to be capable of transporting the Kitchen Gods to heaven.

The days leading up to Tết are also given over to general spring cleaning, both a practical and a meaningful way to clear out the old and get ready for the new. Some families also rid their home of 'unlucky' foods, including dog meat, duck and squid. A food can be considered inauspicious for a number of reasons: its name might be similar to Vietnamese words for things like 'suffer', 'sadness' or 'lack'; or it may have some kind of undesirable symbolic characteristic – squid is out due to the unlucky black of its ink, while shrimp, which swim backwards, are a no-no at a time of year when people are all about moving forwards.

FIVE LUCKY FRUITS

Copious amounts of food are prepared ahead of Tết, including sticky rice cakes for eating and gifting, and trays of five fruits to represent the five wishes for the new year: wealth, prosperity, longevity, health and peace. Selections vary regionally, but some fruits are particularly popular due to their auspicious qualities. These include pomegranates (the seeds represent a family with many children); bunches of bananas or Buddha's hand fruit (which resembles a protective hand); mangoes (xoài in Vietnamese, favoured due to the similarity of their name to the word for 'spend', xài*); watermelon (propitiously round and red) and persimmons (the rosy, fleshy colour represents health and wealth).*

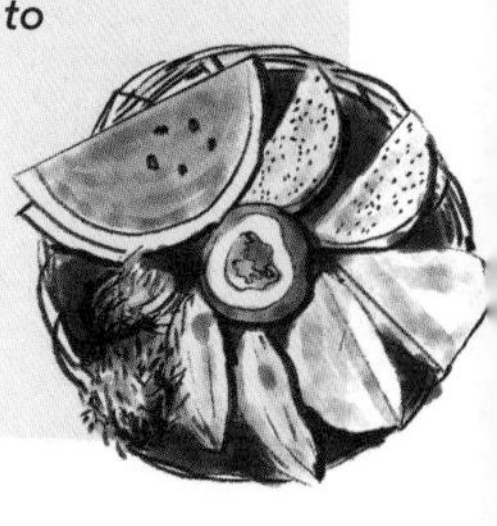

© Walter Bibikow / AWL Images

Above: Tết decorations in Hanoi
Below: Street celebrations to mark the Lunar New Year

© salajean / Getty Images

TẾT FOR TRAVELLERS

Vietnam more or less comes to a standstill during Tết, as cities empty out and people return to their home towns to be with family. For many, it's at least a week-long affair. If you're in Vietnam for an extended period, the relaxed atmosphere, quiet streets and spontaneous invitations to join in the fun are hugely enjoyable. But Tết is not the ideal time to travel around Vietnam: transportation gets sold out months in advance, hotels charge a premium, local attractions are closed, and you'll probably have to settle for Western-style fast food until the restaurants and markets open up again.

TẾT WISHES

Happy New Year
Chúc mừng năm mới - júhk moo·ùhng nuhm mer·eé

May all your wishes come true
Vạn sự như ý - vaạn sẹrh nyuhr eé

I wish you good health in the New Year
Năm mới dồi dào sức khỏe - nuhm mer·eé zoy zow súhrk kwả

May the New Year bring peace and health to your whole family
Năm mới toàn gia bình an - nuhm mer·eé taa·aàng zaa bìng aan

May you live to be a hundred years old *(for older people)*
Chúc bác sống lâu trăm tuổi - júhk baák sóm loh chuhm too·eẻ

Eat lots and grow up fast *(for kids)*
Chúc hay ăn chóng lớn - júhk hay uhn jóm érn

May you soon find yourself a significant other *(for single people)*
Chúc mau chóng tìm được người yêu - júhk mow jóm dee·ùhm đuhr·ẹrk ngoò·ee ee·oo

May your money come in as fast as the Da River and go out as slowly as a drip of coffee
Tiền vào nhu nước sông Đà, tiền ra nhỏ giọt như cà phê phin - dee·ùhn vow nyuhr nuhr·érk som daa, dee·ùhn raa nyỏ zọt nyuhr ğaà fe feen

© kokkai / Getty Images

OFFERINGS AND PRAYERS

Tết is a time for Vietnamese families to remember their ancestors. Many get together to visit, tidy up and add flowers to the graves of parents, grandparents and other relatives; it's also common to burn incense and say prayers to the ancestors, asking them for help to make the upcoming year a successful one.

On the eve of Tết, at the family dinner, a tray of food will be laid out for deceased ancestors; many also set up a table just outside the home (where heaven and earth meet) laden with fruit, incense, candles, betel nut, boiled chicken, sticky rice cakes and tea, rice wine or cans of beer. At the stroke of midnight, the head of the family will say a prayer to the gods here and plant an incense stick into a bowl of uncooked rice; another prayer is then intoned inside the home to the ancestors, in front of an altar where similar offerings have been placed. Finally, Tết wishes are exchanged in a ceremonial letting go of all the bad things from the previous year, and in anticipation of a better year ahead.

© HuyThoai / Getty Images

© Daniel William / Shutterstock

Opposite: Ho Chi Minh City during Tết
Left: Temple offerings
Below: Preparing calligraphy gifts for Tết

CELEBRATING TẾT

The first day of the New Year is reserved for family. Children dressed in crisp new clothes wish parents and grandparents a long life, while adults give kids little red *lì xì* envelopes of money, with wishes for them to grow bigger, study well and be happy.

In the next few days, some families will go to a pagoda to show respect to Buddha and their ancestors, as well as to pray for luck and prosperity. Since everyone is back in their home towns, it's also a good time to catch up with old friends, neighbours and teachers, as well as play games, sing karaoke (preferably very badly yet very loudly, a deadly combination) and, of course, eat and drink to oblivion.

TẾT TIPS

There are a lot of superstitions surrounding Tết, and these essential dos and don'ts will help to navigate the festivities.

DO

- **Wear brightly coloured clothing.** *White and black are taboo, as they're the colours of funeral attire.*
- **Be careful not to break anything,** *including dishes or glasses; doing so is a bad omen, which may point to the breaking of family ties.*
- **Give gifts,** *including red and yellow flowers, health-giving products like swallows' nests or reishi mushrooms (but not medicine), and imported wine or beer.*

DON'T

- **Sweep the house during the first three days of Tết.** *The Vietnamese believe that this will sweep away good luck.*
- **Be the first visitor during Tết.** *Vietnamese will carefully select a very successful or otherwise lucky person to be the first caller of the New Year, in hope of their fortune carrying over to the family – so don't make house calls without an invitation.*
- **Borrow or lend money.** *Borrowing money during Tết means you'll be poor for the rest of the year, while lending is akin to giving away good fortune.*

Above: Apricot blossoms for Tết
Below: Giac Vien pagoda in HCMC

© HuyThoai / Getty Images

© ThuTruong / Getty Images

Above: Dragon dancers often feature in Tết celebrations

© Phuong-Thao / Shutterstock

A BLOOMING NEW YEAR

In the weeks leading up to Tết, the streets of Vietnam are resplendent with flowers: red blooms symbolising luck, and yellow representing gold or wealth. In the north, the red is chiefly represented by (pink) peach blossoms, along with crimson-hued daises, roses and poinsettias. In the south, the preferred yellow bloom is apricot blossom, though chrysanthemums, sunflowers and marigolds (the latter being both yellow and long-lasting, representing longevity) are also popular.

In a bid to surround themselves with signs of fertility and bounty for the New Year, private homes are also decorated with flowering plants, as well as small fruit trees bearing kumquats, cluster figs, pomelos and dragon fruit, to name just a few. Ensuring that the plants are bursting with fruit and blossoms just in time for Tết requires a certain skill – along with the use of fertilisers, hormones and insecticides.

For the Vietnamese, spring flowers contrast old age and eventual death with the never-ending cycle of life. As Tết is a celebration of spring and new life, citrus trees are prized because they're able to bloom and bear fruit in the cold of winter, while the peach is one of the first trees to come to life, its delicate pink flowers a sure harbinger of spring.

Nowadays, especially in the south, the Vietnamese like to decorate their homes with potted apricot trees. There's an entire industry centred around looking after these trees year-round, and making sure they come into full bloom just in time for Tết. For those who can't afford to buy their own high-end tree outright (they can be hugely expensive), or who aren't prepared to take care of a tree year-round simply to enjoy its beauty for a couple of weeks, many Tết flower specialists offer apricot tree rentals, complete with delivery, set up and pick-up after the holidays.

THE LEGEND OF THE APRICOT TREE

In the south, Tết's association with apricot blossoms has its origin in a Vietnamese folk tale about a father and daughter who set out to slay a python-like monster. In order to be able to see her from afar, the girl's mother made her a bright yellow tunic. But though the girl managed to kill the monster in the ensuing battle, it also crushed her to death. Witnessing the tragic scene, the Jade Emperor decided to give the brave girl life, but only for nine days every year around the time of the Tết festival. Though saddened by grief, the family found comfort in the thought of her returning every year. When the parents grew old and died, the girl was turned into an apricot tree by the family altar; during the precious few days at Tết, the tree blossoms, cloaked in a yellow as bright as the tunic that the girl wore in life.

Tết Foods and Their Meanings

Many of the foods eaten during Tết are popular year-round, but these special dishes are always a part of the celebrations.

© Pham Le Huong Son / Getty Images

Caramelised pork with eggs *(thịt kho tàu)*
Braised chunks of caramelised pork belly with hardboiled eggs; coconut water and palm sugar in the sauce add sweetness, and a side of pickled leeks helps to cut down the richness of the pork. Thanks to the caramelisation, *thịt kho tàu* lasts a long time, so can be called upon for a fast, easy meal over the holidays. The square chunks of meat and the round eggs convey a harmony of yin and yang.

© trangiap / Getty Images

Candied fruit and nuts
Candied fruits, nuts and seeds are chosen for their auspicious colour – yellow kumquats, red watermelon or cherry tomatoes – or for what they represent. Peanuts are known as the 'longevity nut', while lotus seeds are a symbol of a houseful of children and grandchildren. On a practical side, these little snacks come in handy when guests stop by during the holidays; they're usually enjoyed with hot tea.

© AnnaPustynnikova / Getty Images

Sticky rice cakes *(bánh chưng* and *bánh tét)*
The square *bánh chưng* and round *bánh tét* are said to represent earth and heaven. Filled with mung beans and pork, these cakes take hours to cook over a traditional wood fire, which provides the perfect family bonding activity - time to chat and tell stories. They can be made in advance and be left out for weeks without refrigeration, making them the perfect no-fuss Tết food.

THE TẾT DINNER

A bountiful meal with the family (and the spirits of the ancestors) is an essential part of Tết celebrations, and typically comprises four bowls and four plates, neatly presented on a round tray for everyone to share – the number four represents the four seasons and four directions. The food varies from region to region, and many homes won't have all eight dishes, but a typical tray might include bowls of sautéed kohlrabi and three soups (perhaps made with dried pork skin, with bamboo shoots and pigs' feet, or with mushrooms with pork meatballs). The plates are piled with chicken, jellied pork, lean pork ham and a sticky rice cake.

© Tony albelton / Shutterstock

Boiled chicken *(gà luộc)* The vibrant yellow colour of boiled chicken signifies wealth and plenty.

© bonchan / Shutterstock

Bitter gourd soup *(khổ qua nhồi thịt)* Traditionally, sweet foods are preferred at Tết, but this soup of bitter gourd stuffed with minced pork is just the opposite. It's a Tết favourite due to a play on words with its name, which can also mean 'suffering gone' – the Vietnamese eat it in hopes that the problems and miseries of the previous year will fade away.

© Ho Su A Bi / Shutterstock

Jellied pork *(thịt đông)* A terrine combining pork meat with cartilage, hocks, feet, tails and ears, which release their natural gelatine during the cooking process and create the terrine's jelly. Carrots and wood-ear mushrooms give some colour, and the terrine is sliced and eaten cold. The harmony of the many ingredients is said to represent a close-knit family, while the clear jelly symbolises hope for the coming year.

Bánh Chưng and Bánh Giầy

Choice delicacies are often called the 'food of the gods' – but these Vietnamese rice flour cakes are - in legend, at least - foods of the fairies.

PARCELS OF PERFECTION

These sticky rice flour cakes are made from simple ingredients that are meaningful to the Vietnamese: glutinous rice, mung beans and pork belly, seasoned with fish sauce and black pepper and wrapped in banana leaves which impart a greenish tint. A wooden mould is used to give *bánh chưng* its distinctive square shape; after being trussed with bamboo strips, the parcels are boiled for 10 to 12 hours, then pressed to drain and help maintain their shape. Circular *bánh giầy* are even more simple – a gloopy batter of powdered glutinous rice, salt and water that's steamed on a bed of banana leaves, and eaten with a slice of lean pork ham and a sprinkle of salt and pepper.

Legendary associations aside, *bánh chưng* are popular during Tết because of their time-consuming production process. Fussing over ingredients (fancier Tết fillings include cashews or dried shrimp) and pulling all-nighters to tend to wood fires requires a team effort – the perfect excuse for families to spend time together.

Supermarkets or corner shops sell *bánh chưng* and *bánh giầy* year-round. They're usually eaten for breakfast, and paired with something sour to cut through the heaviness of the rice – perhaps pickled white radishes. Prettily wrapped *bánh chưng* make a nice Tết gift, but should always be presented in pairs rather than singly.

THE LEGEND OF THE STICKY RICE FLOUR CAKES

According to Vietnamese culinary lore, the story of bánh chưng *and* bánh giầy *has its origins in the time of the Hồng Bàng dynasty, a (probably legendary) lineage said to have ruled Vietnam from 2879 BCE to 258 BCE. To resolve the dilemma of which of his 18 sons should succeed him, Emperor Hùng presented them with a foodie challenge: whichever prince was able to present a dish that was both delicious and meaningful would inherit the throne.*

*Most of the princes travelled widely in their search for fantastic dishes never before seen in Vietnam. But the youngest one, Tiết Liêu, was also the humblest, and opted to carry out his quest close to home. In a dream, he saw a fairy who told him that there was nothing more valuable in heaven and on earth than rice, source of nourishment for the people. The fairy instructed him to make two cakes, one square to represent the earth, and one round for heaven. She told him to fill them with beans and meat and to wrap them with leaves, representing the loving arms of parents protecting their children. When he woke, Tiết Liêu set about finding the best quality glutinous rice he could, and made a square cake (*bánh chưng*) and a round cake (*bánh giầy*).*

Having completed their mission, the princes presented their fantastical finds to Emperor Hùng. Tiết Liêu's humble cakes seemed lowly offerings compared to the rare and delicious treats of his brothers, but having heard of the dream and tasted the cakes, Emperor Hùng gave the throne to Tiết Liêu. And the rest, as they say, is history.

© Thang Tat Nguyen / Getty Images

Above: Preparing *bánh chưng*

THE RICE COOKING FESTIVAL AT THỊ CẤM VILLAGE

Vietnam celebrates many food-related festivities, but few can match the history and tradition of Thị Cấm's Rice Cooking Festival, staged on the eighth day of Tết in a small village that's around an hour's drive west of central Hanoi.

According to legend, Phan Tây Nhạc, a general of the 18th Hùng king, first held rice cooking competitions here to test the skill of the soldiers he had stationed at Thị Cấm. Following the general's death, the villagers adopted him as their spirit protector and carried on his tradition.

On the day, four teams of ten compete, comprised of men and women, boys and girls. Young boys run the short distance to the Nhuệ River to fetch water, while the strongest team members light the fires by hand using straw kindling, a long piece of bamboo and a bamboo strap with handles at each end, which is pulled back and forth to create a spark. The rice is then threshed in a stone mortar – skill and brute force are needed to separate the grains from the chaff without breaking the rice into bits. The grains are then carefully winnowed and washed, to ensure a snowy white colour and dispense with remaining grit and husks. In the final stage, village women cook the rice in earthenware pots over the fires, making sure to keep the heat even and placing straw ash around the pots to finish the cooking. Large ceremonial drums and raucous cheers from the crowd add to the fervour.

The four rice pots then go to the judges, usually the village elders. They carefully taste each pot of rice and crown the winning team based on the colour, fragrance and texture of the rice. The winning entry is placed on the altar to the village deity, tasked with protecting the village from harm. The whole affair is frenzied, loud and very smoky, but steeped in colourful culture and tradition.

WHERE TO EAT AND DRINK

A FOODIE HOTSPOT

Take a tour of any Vietnamese city and you'll quickly discover why this is one of the world's top foodie spots. In virtually any urban area it's hard to walk for more than a couple of minutes without passing a glass case filled with freshly baked baguettes ready to be stuffed with fried eggs or cold cuts, a push-cart loaded with jellies and puddings, or a roadside charcoal BBQ wafting out wonderful aromas of lemongrass and marinated pork. And making the meals that bit sweeter is the fact that most of these delicious treats cost US$1 or less.

Life in Vietnam is lived out on the streets, meaning good eats are accessible at practically any time of the day or night. Morning commuters might devour a container of ready-made fried rice or stir-fried noodles bought from a streetside cart without ever dismounting from their motorbike; those with a little more time can sit down to a batch of still-steaming rice-flour rolls stuffed with minced pork and mushrooms, or perhaps a bowl of noodle soup topped with wontons and slices of char siu pork.

Street food aside, Vietnam offers plenty of other eating options. Cafés – busy from mid-morning onwards – do great bubble tea as well as coffees, while lunchtime sees office crowds pouring out of their buildings in search of sustenance, perhaps at a trendy diner offering inexpensive set lunches. Lunchtime is also when vendors start setting up around schools and universities, selling quick, cheap meals of fried rice or noodles to hungry students.

As the day wears on (and especially at weekends), families come out in droves to feast. BBQ joints, hot-pot restaurants and beer gardens come alive with friends clinking glasses to loud toasts of '*Một, hai, ba, vô!*' (one, two, three, drink!'), while happily munching on snacks like chicken feet or grilled squid. Even late into the night, when most establishments have closed, listen carefully and you might hear the light rhythmic tapping sound which signals that a mobile noodle vendor is open for business, ready to deliver to your door. Wherever you are, whatever the time of day, there are some seriously good eats to be had in Vietnam.

Right: Lunch on the go for a Hue market trader

PLACES TO EAT

Vietnam offers a host of informal eating options, from mom-and-dad street stalls to simple *quán ăn* places offering quick and easy lunch or dinner.

THE VIETNAMESE 'POP-UP'

Vietnam is a nation of excellent cooks, and many show off their kitchen skills via the informal single-dish outfits that pop up in urban areas at set times of the day. In the mornings, practically every neighbourhood will have a few of these, identifiable by some kind of glass case and a makeshift sign propped at the side of the road or down an alleyway. Add in something to cook on (usually a charcoal brazier or portable gas stove), an umbrella for shade and a table and low plastic stools for customers and the 'pop-up' is complete.

Above: A pop-up street cafe at breakfast time

These informal diners are often staffed by women looking to earn some extra income while working close to (often in front of) their homes or on an empty stretch of pavement. They tend to specialise in simple one-dish meals like noodle soup, a plate of *cơm tấm* (broken rice topped with a char-grilled pork chop) or a steamed egg quiche with minced pork. Husbands will sometimes pitch in by grilling the pork before they head off to work, or grandparents might collect the money and bundle items for take-away, but often it's just one hardworking woman waking up very early to get everything ready, and then selling her dish until it runs out (usually by mid-morning)

In the late afternoon or evening, stalls are also set up to catch students and commuters on their way home: look for a crowd or bunch of

WHAT'S IN A NAME?

While both quán *and* nhà hàng *are usually translated as 'restaurant', they're not quite the same.* Nhà hàng *are full-service restaurants with a proper menu, ranging from family-friendly eateries to fine dining places, while* quán *are smaller establishments with just a few seats and a limited menu, sometimes just one dish. A* quán cà-phê *will offer coffee and maybe very simple meals or snacks, while a* quán phở *will only serve Vietnam's signature noodle soup, and a* quán bánh xèo *just savoury pork- and shrimp-stuffed crepes. The latter two dishes are typically too fussy to make at home – phở requires lots of cooking time, while* bánh xèo *demands lots of ingredients and a superheated wok – most people leave it to the* quán.

© Bruno De Hogues / Getty Images

Above: Hmong diners at Can Cau market, northern Vietnam

motorbikes parked along the road, and expect such delights as egg noodles with sliced pork, stir-fried crispy noodles or fried rice, all cooked up over a roaring fire.

QUÁN ĂN

The most common type of informal eatery are *quán ăn*, simple places doling out servings of pre-prepared local staples, and identifiable by a big glass case with a sign that says 'cơm' out front (*cơm* literally translates as rice, but can also mean meals in a broader sense). The case holds trays of freshly made food such as caramelised pork with hard-boiled eggs, some kind of vegetable stir-fry with meat, and a soup – perhaps bitter melon stuffed with minced pork or a sweet-and-sour broth loaded with tomatoes, pineapple, okra and fish.

Ordering couldn't be easier – it's just a matter of pointing to what you want and sitting down. Just the right amount will be brought to your table, tailored to how many people are eating. There's no menu and no price list, and tea and extra rice are often included. At the end of the meal, someone will come over, check out your empty plates, remember what you had and give you a price. To ensure the freshest food possible, aim to beat the rush by getting there before peak times: 11am/11.30am to avoid the lunch crowd or, for places offering dinner, 4pm/4.30pm, before homeward-bound office workers descend. Be wary, however, of *quán ăn* close to bus and train stations; their clientele is transitory, and without repeat guests to worry about, the food can sometimes be poor quality and overpriced.

© Yvan Cohen / Getty Images

Above: Serving up lunch at a typical *quán ăn*

Below: Alfresco dining is huge in Hanoi

© Bruno De Hogues / Getty Images

Ready-made food from large supermarkets can be an even more economical way of eating. Some items (spring rolls with rice noodles, chicken and rice) may be pre-packaged, but most dishes are charged by weight, then packaged in small plastic bags, ready to take away.

CƠM VĂN PHÒNG

These three simple words, which literally translate as 'meals for office workers', signify some of the best deals around. Available only at lunch and usually in more urbanised areas, a *cơm văn phòng* is a complete three-course meal comprising small portions of a main dish (maybe stewed pork ribs or fried fish with shredded mango), plus a simple soup and a vegetable dish, typically stir-fried. At some places you'll have multiple options for each course, while at others you're served whatever the cook has made that day. Trendy café-lounges which normally serve fancy coffees for US$2–3 often drum up lunchtime custom by offering *cơm văn phòng* for the same price as a coffee.

SHARING CUISINES – HOT POTS AND BARBECUE

For the Vietnamese, meal times are social occasions, which explains the popularity of

Above: Chic kerbside dining near the Hoi An waterfront

© Jordan Banks / FCR

hot-pot (*lẩu*) and barbecue (*nướng*) restaurants, where everyone pitches in to cook the meal. At hot-pot places, start by picking your broth - spicy Thai-style or fermented fish-paste-based versions are popular. The broth will be brought to the table atop a portable stove (in more modern restaurants, the heating element will be built into the table), where it's used to cook the other ingredients: fresh veg and herbs, proteins (sliced beef, meatballs, shrimp, squid and fish are common) and rice or egg noodles (and sometimes instant noodles) to add some filling bulk. Everyone pitches in to put ingredients into the broth, and to keep a watchful eye for when things are cooked. It's the ultimate sharing experience, a little bit like Swiss fondue but with lots more chopsticks, elbows and vegetables.

Barbecue restaurants are similar - a plate of meat or fish and vegetables are brought to the table to be cooked atop a charcoal brazier that's been smeared with lard or butter. Trying to avoid the eyewatering smoke is just part of the fun. The pacing of the meal is key here, as some meats cook more quickly than others, so it requires some skill to put just enough on the grill to keep the meal and the conversation going without ending up with a cold pile of cooked items.

In both types of restaurants, waiters will be on hand to add more fuel if needed or turn off the stove when the meal winds down; you can also order more of any single item if the default selection isn't enough.

SEAFOOD RESTAURANTS

Known as *quán ốc* (*ốc* means snail or mollusc), these informal seafood eateries are especially popular in the evenings. Look for large buckets or stacked trays filled with clams, scallops, oysters and other seafood; some places also have tanks with live specimens ready for the picking. While some smaller dishes have fixed prices, you'll usually be given a per-kilo price for whatever you point to – this is market rate, plus a little extra for cooking the food to your liking. Steaming with lemongrass or beer is popular, as is stir-frying with strands of fresh peppercorns or fried garlic. For a real taste bomb, try getting shrimp or crab flash-fried with tamarind, which makes a wonderfully tangy, gooey sauce. Most *quán ốc* don't serve rice; the food is meant to be eaten as is, washed down with some cold beer. Don't worry about getting your hands dirty – it's all part of the allure, and moist towelettes or finger bowls are provided. Snail meat can be deceptively hard to get at – that's what the toothpicks are for.

QUÁN NHẬU

The Vietnamese are the second most prolific drinkers of beer in Asia, and like to accompany it with some good food – enter the *quán nhậu*, or beer gardens. 'Nhậu' is notoriously hard to translate in English: it connotes social drinking, but more on the side of low-key eating and drinking than heavy partying. Typically in an open-air setting (though with shade and rain cover), *quán nhậu* are welcoming to families, despite the rather incongruous pairing of kids with sometimes raucous inebriates and the sash-clad 'beer girls' promoting the latest offerings from breweries. Often equipped with big-screen TVs, *quán nhậu* double as sports bars, especially when Vietnam is playing an international football match.

Rather than being filling, *nhậu* cuisine is about complementing the taste of beer and making the diner feel thirsty (and so drink more). Expect lots of meat-heavy dishes made without oil and sauces, like dried squid, grilled shrimp skewers and barbecued beef. Salty and sour dishes include roasted peanuts, little leaf-wrapped packets of fermented pork ham, or deep-fried tofu dipped in fermented shrimp paste; crunchy chicken feet and crispy sesame crackers are other typical offerings.

© Evgenii Mitroshin / Getty Images

Left: A street seafood restaurant in Ho Chi Minh City

VIETNAM'S FASTER FOOD

Opposite: Fast food, Vietnam-style

Vietnam is one of the world's street-food hotspots, but big-name international chains have moved in nonetheless, with varying degrees of success.

There's no shame in craving a taste of home during your travels around Vietnam – noodles for breakfast isn't for everyone, even if these are some of the world's best noodles. And there's probably a limit to how much rice, rice paper, rice-flour rolls, rice noodles and other rice products that someone who grew up with bread and potatoes can take.

There are a fair few international fast-food chains in Vietnam doling out burgers, pizza, fried chicken and the like. With its huge young population, growing middle class and affinity for the West, Vietnam would seem like a ripe market for fast food. But despite being present here for many years, and investing heavily in development and marketing, the international chains haven't really been embraced by the Vietnamese. According to data from the European Commission, only 1% of the money spent on food by the average Vietnamese goes on international-style fast food, while a whopping 78% is spent at local stalls and sellers. So why hasn't fast food taken off in Vietnam as it has in nearby China and Japan?

IS IT REALLY 'FAST' FOOD?

The whole point of fast food restaurants is convenience – but Vietnamese vendors have fast food restaurants beat. When a steaming bowl of phở or a baguette stuffed with all the fixings takes about a minute to assemble and means no lines to wait in, Vietnamese food is the epitome of fast. Most food joints are also streetside, meaning you just need to pull up on your motorbike and walk over to your seat, rather than find and pay for parking. And where the street food sold in many other countries is more snacks than real food, Vietnam's abundance of streetside eateries often serve complete meals.

SHARING IS CARING

There's a definite social aspect to Vietnamese eating: interacting with the seller, chatting with other customers, eating from the same communal plates with friends and colleagues – all of which is entirely missing from the mechanised assembly-line nature of fast food restaurants. Also, it's pretty hard to share a hamburger.

TRAD LOCAL TASTES

In general, Vietnamese like their food traditional. While burgers, pizzas and fries are undeniably popular with the younger generation, the Vietnamese are used to eating fresh and healthy meals with lots of fresh herbs and greens, rather than calorie-laden, heavy and oily fried foods.

DON'T BELIEVE THE HYPE

When Starbucks opened its first Vietnam outlet in 2013, and McDonald's arrived in 2014, there were queues around the block – people wanted to be among the first to sample these world-renowned brands that came with instant cachet. But in the years since, growth has been much slower than anticipated, in part because many Vietnamese view a McDonald's meal or a cup of Starbucks coffee as a splurge, reserved for date night or a kids' birthday party, rather than a part of their regular routine.

© Bruno De Hogues / Getty Images

LOCALS DO IT BETTER AND CHEAPER

The Vietnamese are spoilt for choice when it comes to food done quickly, so it's understandable that most don't choose to limit themselves to choosing between burgers and chicken. The locals also do fast food more cheaply: the price of a Big Mac and a five-dollar coffee is the equivalent of half a day's salary, while a bánh mì sandwich loaded with all the fillings costs a quarter of that. And paying a premium for fancy coffees seems ridiculous given the fact that Vietnam is the world's second-largest producer of coffee beans. The Vietnamese have an apt saying, 'Chở củi về rừng', which translates to 'transporting wood back to the forest'.

Above: A bowl of phở for breakfast in Lao Cai, northwest Vietnam

TIPS FOR EATING OUT

Eating out in Vietnam is generally relaxed and straightforward, a happy free-for-all where everyone's main concern is having a good time. However, there are a few etiquette basics to be aware of.

THERE ARE NO COURSES

Unless you're in a true fine dining establishment (typically in a high-end hotel) or having a set meal, the dishes will arrive at the table as soon as they're cooked – this also applies in larger restaurants which segment menus into appetisers, soups and mains. And it's not unusual for the communal bowl of rice to come out last, as an apparent afterthought to the food – just dig in as soon as the dishes start coming out.

IT'S A SHARED AFFAIR

Most Vietnamese meals are meant for sharing, with the exception of one-dish noodle soups like phở or plates that come with individual rice portions. Otherwise, ordering shared plates is the norm, with everyone at the table working together to make sure all the food groups are covered and there's a good balance of flavours.

DRINKING ETIQUETTE

When Vietnamese go drinking ('đi nhậu'), the fun only stops when everyone's drunk or at least tipsy. When one person drinks, everyone else is expected to follow suit; and if your glass is half full, someone will feel obliged to top it up – not doing so is considered rude. Throughout the night, glasses will be clinked dozens of times: a shouted toast of 'một, hai, ba, vô!' is the cue to take another swig. As a non-Vietnamese guest, you can be exempted from alcohol by saying 'Tôi không biết uống' (literally, 'I don't know how to drink'), but to avoid putting a damper on the jovial mood, order something soft and drink along with everyone else.

WHO'S PAYING?

The question of who picks up the tab is a tricky one. In Vietnamese, there are two ways of saying 'invite': *rủ* and *mời*. *Rủ* is used amongst friends, as per 'let's check out this new restaurant'; *mời* indicates that you're being formally invited and shouldn't think about trying to pay (doing so would be an affront to the person who invited you). Friends or acquaintances sometimes clarify what the intention is by asking 'rủ hay mời?'; if in doubt, be quick to take out your wallet when the bill comes – it's likely to be waved away, but the gesture will be appreciated. At the end of a group meal, it's highly unusual (and considered crass) to calculate what's individually owed; usually, group members take turns to pick up the whole tab.

TIPPING AND WAITSTAFF

Some high-end restaurants include VAT and a service charge in the bill, but Vietnam doesn't have a tipping culture per se – there's no expected percentage at the end of a meal. Tipping is not expected at street stalls or smaller eateries with no wait staff (though if you arrive by motorbike, you might give a small tip to the security guard). Many Vietnamese do leave the change from the bill at mid-priced restaurants – but bear in mind that as waiting staff are paid well under US$1 an hour, the level of service may not be on a par with that in more developed countries. It's usual in Vietnam to get your server's attention during the meal with a wave of the hand or, if addressing someone younger than you, by saying 'em ơi!'.

Above: Pavement fruit and veg stall in Hoi An

VEGETARIAN AND VEGAN VIETNAM

According to the Vietnamese proverb, 'a meal without vegetables is like being sick with no medicine', and meat-free food is central to the national cuisine.

© hadynyah / Getty Images

Above: Colourful produce at a Mekong Delta floating market

VEGETARIAN FOOD

From the stacks of fresh herbs and lettuce piled onto noodle soup to vegetables stir-fried as a side dish, or carrots, turnips and baby aubergines (eggplants) pickled as a condiment, vegetables are a big part of Vietnamese cuisine. A sizeable portion of Vietnamese practise Buddhism, Hoahaosim and Caodaism, religions that discourage the killing and eating of animals. Vietnam's Buddhists (about 10% of the population) aren't all lifelong vegetarians, but most abstain from meat on certain days of the lunar month (usually around the first and fifteenth), and some restaurants switch to an all-vegetarian menu on those days. Tradition also dictates eating vegetarian fare around certain important life events, such as mourning a close family member. All these factors combine to make Vietnam a vegetarian-friendly destination in many ways.

Because many Vietnamese meals are assembled piecemeal, as per the various fillings that go into a bánh mì, it's easy to avoid meat by simply pointing to what you don't want and shaking 'no' with your hand or forefinger.

Right: A mobile market in Hanoi's Old Quarter

© kitzcorner / Shutterstock

Eateries that serve ready-made dishes will always have a selection of veggie options – but note that these will probably include fish sauce. While you can tell your waiter 'Tôi ăn chay' ('I'm a vegetarian'), they may not understand; and as eggs or fish sauce are often assumed to be fine for vegetarians, chefs won't always accommodate requests despite the best of intentions.

VEGAN FOOD

There is a Vietnamese word for veganism – *thuần chay* – but as a concept it hasn't really caught on. In most restaurants, the only way to ensure that you get vegan food is to specify exactly what you don't eat, perhaps by presenting a written list. Happily, other than meat and fish sauce, most Vietnamese dishes don't incorporate animal products,

Below: Plant-based heaven in a tofu summer roll

© Daniel Keuck / Alamy Stock Photo

using coconut milk instead of cow's milk or 'butter' made from oil rather than milk. Vietnamese are also not big on cheese. Foods to be wary of include fruit shakes (which usually contain condensed milk) and sweet teas (sometimes made with honey); coffee is often served with condensed milk, and sometimes the beans are treated with butter or even fish sauce to remove bitterness.

EATING OUT

Dedicated vegan restaurants are extremely rare, but urban areas will likely have a selection of vegetarian restaurants and street food stalls – just look for the adjective 'chay' in the name; regular restaurants list non-meat options such as veggie noodle soup as *phở chay*

Above: Lunch from Hanoi vegetarian specialist Pi Bistro

© Pi Bistro

or *hủ tiếu chay*. Designated vegetarian restaurants might have a sign that reads *quán chay* or *cơm chay*, and use veggie stocks for soups, vegetarian fish sauce and oyster sauce, and delicious, local plant-based ingredients like shiitake and king oyster mushrooms, crunchy lotus stems and roots, and all manner of tofu and noodles.

On the minus side, instead of celebrating the natural flavours of vegetables, many vegetarian restaurants cater to nominal (read: unenthusiastic) vegetarians, putting a lot of effort into making vegetarian dishes look and taste like their meaty counterparts with the use of tofu and various starches shaped to look like shrimp or pork, or using packaged mock meats that sacrifice taste and texture for appearance. A few standout vegetarian restaurants have gained strong followings for really showcasing vegetarian fare in innovative ways; in Ho Chi Minh City there's Hum (three locations) and Pi Bistro, while Hanoi has Uu Dam and Aummee. A good way of finding vegetarian restaurants (which cluster around Buddhist spaces) is to search for a temple or pagoda close to where you are via Google Maps, then zoom in to see if there are any nearby restaurants with the word 'chay' in the name.

GLUTEN-FREE VIETNAM

Given rice is the national carb, much of Vietnamese cuisine is unintentionally gluten-free, though there are a few possible pitfalls.

GLUTEN-FREE FOODS

Vietnam has a much lower instance of coeliac disease than in Western societies, perhaps because the national cuisine doesn't employ much wheat, barley and rye by its very nature. As a result, there's little general awareness of gluten intolerance.

However, because rice and everything rice-related dominates in Vietnam - rice paper, flour, noodles, vermicelli, congee and so forth - you can eat very well without having to limit yourself too much. Other common ingredients that happen to be gluten-free include tapioca and most fish sauces. Locally made soy sauce typically does not contain wheat, though fancier restaurants might use imported seasoning products that do.

FOODS TO WATCH OUT FOR

The word for wheat in Vietnamese is *lúa mì*. To further confuse the issue, *mì* also means noodles that are typically not made from rice, and which may or may not contain gluten. (The exception is *mì quảng*, yellowish rice noodles coloured with turmeric.) Processed meats, including local sausages and pâté, may also include wheat or soy sauce. Fried spring rolls can either be wrapped in rice paper or a wheat-based pastry-like sheet. Rice-paper-wrapped spring rolls have a thinner skin which is less even in texture and may have a few bubbles.

OTHER GLUTEN-CONTAINING FOODS INCLUDE:

Bánh mì *The classic Vietnamese sandwich is always made with wheat-flour baguettes (sometimes with the addition of rice flour in the bread dough).*

Mì *Also spelled* mỳ, *these yellow egg and wheat noodles are widely used in soups and stir-fries.*

Nui *Pasta, most often macaroni-like tubes used in soups and stir-fried with beef. The yellow ones are made from wheat, though there is a white, rice-flour based kind.*

© rez-art / Getty Images

Above: Gluten-free rice noodles are a Vietnamese staple

Above: A list of your allergies can help when buying food in markets

FOOD ALLERGIES

Food allergies are not common in Vietnam, so awareness among kitchen staff and servers is low. You'll need to be very proactive in order to ensure that you don't eat foods containing allergens, and may have to forgo a lot of the street food.

AVOIDING ALLERGENS

While asking about ingredients and communicating what you can or cannot eat is your first line of defence, staff may not understand you (a written card in Vietnamese is helpful), and may not be familiar with the potential consequences of eating allergens. And as cross-contamination is common in Vietnamese kitchens, travellers with life-threatening allergies might choose to eat only at restaurants and hotels used to dealing with foreigners, or simply prepare their own food. In all cases, being proactive and vigilant is your best defence.

Potential allergens

DAIRY

Many Asians are lactose intolerant and in general, Vietnamese don't consume a lot of dairy products. The most common forms of dairy that you'll encounter are condensed milk (found in iced coffees, smoothies and ice-cream) and milk products found in some white breads.

SOY

Soy beans figure heavily in Vietnamese food, from sweetened soy milk to tofu to soy sauce. Soy-bean oil is also used.

EGGS

Chicken, duck and quail eggs are commonly used in Vietnamese food. Fried eggs frequently top a plate of grilled pork and rice or get stuffed into a baguette, while hard-boiled eggs typically accompany caramelised pork. Most yellow noodles contain eggs.

NUTS AND SEEDS

Nuts and seeds are common in Vietnamese cuisine, especially peanuts and sesame. You'll find crushed and roasted peanuts in *nước chấm* and hoisin sauces; they're also added to salads as a final garnish, and even appear in drinks (like tamarind juice) and desserts (such as the pudding-like *chè*). Sesame seeds are also sprinkled on top of salads, and sesame oil is common in stir-fried dishes. It's rare to find nut products in soups (with the exception of the peanuts which top *mì quảng* noodle soup). While not as common as other edible oils due to its higher cost, peanut oil is sometimes used in Vietnamese cooking.

FISH AND SHELLFISH

With thousands of kilometres of coastline, the Vietnamese are big seafood eaters. Thankfully, most dishes are clearly labelled when it comes to protein. Other dishes which often contain shrimp are the crispy *bánh xèo* crepes, and fresh summer rolls (in which you'll be able to see the shrimp through the translucent rice paper). Fancier restaurants may also include shrimp or crab in their deep-fried spring rolls.

VIETNAM'S FUSION FOOD

Traditional Vietnamese cuisine has been enlivened by a wave of restaurants that bring local flair to classic fare.

Above: KOTO's signature burger is inspired by the flavours of *bò lá lốt*

After a thousand years of Chinese rule and a hundred years under the French, it's no surprise that many quintessentially Vietnamese dishes are classic fusion foods. The de facto national dish, phở noodle soup, is a perfect example: clear beef broth from the French and handmade noodles from the Chinese, all topped off by Vietnamese-style fresh herbs and sprouts.

INTERNATIONAL OFFERINGS

Modern-day Vietnam has its fair share of international restaurants, especially in urban areas with Korean, Japanese, French and North American expat communities. There are also eateries aimed more to the local market, selling inexpensive Vietnamese versions of pasta or burgers, and streetside carts churning out everything from sushi and takoyaki to fried chicken and doner kebabs. However, fusion cuisine has not yet been widely embraced by many Vietnamese, who tend to like their food more traditional. The restaurants that do fusion food have mainly been foreign-run establishments, aimed at expats and visitors who want to experience Vietnamese flavours wrapped up in familiar foods.

Above: Gourmet fusion from Tam Le's Saigonita pop-up

Courtesy of Pizza 4P's

Courtesy of KOTO

FUSION RESTAURANTS

Pizza 4P's *An expat favourite is the Japanese-owned Pizza 4P's (with locations in Hanoi, Ho Chi Minh City, Danang and Nha Trang), known for their innovative wood-fired pizzas utilising cheeses made near Dalat. Novel pairings incorporating local flavours include the Cơm Tấm Pizza, with grilled pork, pork skin and a fried egg; and the vegan-friendly Lotus Zen, made with soy-milk cheese and lotus root flour and topped with the flower, fruit, stem and crunchy roots from lotus.*

KOTO *KOTO is an acronym for 'Know One, Teach One', and this non-profit social enterprise provides hospitality training for at-risk and disadvantaged Vietnamese youths in its Hanoi and Ho Chi Minh City restaurants. Its signature burger incorporates the flavours of* bò lá lốt *(beef, typically marinated with lemongrass, five-spice powder and soy sauce, wrapped in fragrant leaves and then grilled) with a remoulade of tart star fruit and green papaya.*

VIỆT KIỀU

Vietnam's so-called Việt Kiều chefs are spearheading the country's modern fusion movement. Vietnamese nationals who have lived abroad and returned home to set up exciting new restaurants, the chefs featured here have all made a splash by fusing flavours from their childhood with influences from a variety of world cuisines.

© KEVIN LEE

Above: Lunch at Saigonita

TAM LE

'I grew up on phở and fajitas,' laughs Tam Le, a budding chef whose parents hail from Hue, but who was brought up in Texas, USA. Having found a certain kinship among Mexican friends there, built on similar family-first values and a 'lime and cilantro (coriander)' culinary heritage, Tam made her way back to Vietnam and started the Saigonita pop-up, cooking home-hosted dinners which gained a buzz for their exciting marriage of Mexican and Vietnamese cuisines; classic creations included a take on Hue's steamed *bánh nậm* cakes, using Texan masa and corn husks to wrap up a pork and prawn filling.

'People often talk about authenticity in food, but with food, everyone's borrowing from everyone,' says Le. 'I want more people to rethink what Vietnamese cuisine is. It doesn't have to be cheap or any less complex and respected as, let's say, French cuisine.'

PETER CUONG FRANKLIN

Another Việt Kiều innovator who is taking Vietnamese fusion to a new level is Peter Cuong Franklin, chef-owner of Ho Chi Minh City's renowned Anan Restaurant. In 2017, he made headlines by serving a two-person phở priced at US$100, which consisted of an exemplary French-style consommé loaded with a poached egg, slices of Wagyu, beef ribs cooked sous-vide, a dollop of earthy black truffle paste and a hunk of grilled Australian beef bone sliced in half to reveal the marrow inside, to be scooped out with crispy sesame crackers like a kind of beefy butter.

'If French or Japanese cuisine can be labelled as fine dining, why can't Vietnamese?', asserts Franklin. 'I can make a bowl of phở for US$2 but I can also make it for US$100 to give people who've eaten phở a million times elsewhere a completely new experience.'

LUKE NGUYEN

Trailblazing Vietnamese-Australian chef Luke Nguyen is on a mission to expand perceptions of Vietnamese food and introduce something more upscale and innovative, cooking luxury ingredients in unusual ways. 'Vietnamese food is seen as a cheap meal', he says. 'My parents' generation had their AU$5 phở restaurant, but if we all continue to open that kind of restaurant, Vietnamese food isn't going to get anywhere.' Nguyen has organised fish sauce tastings, and at his Vietnam House restaurant in Ho Chi Minh City, he uses upscale ingredients to make traditional Vietnamese dishes: rice-paper rolls filled with sesame-seared salmon and salmon caviar, or *bánh xèo* pancakes filled with crab meat and Iberico pork. 'I had a struggle when I opened Red Lantern [his acclaimed Sydney restaurant], using premium products like Australian Wagyu and organic produce to bring Vietnamese food to another level where people could match food with wine and take Vietnamese cuisine seriously. Unfortunately, Vietnamese food was always perceived as being cheap, and people were asking, "Why should I pay AUD$17 for a plate of Vietnamese food?" That's the perception I want to change. It starts with paying for and using good ingredients to get a better product.'

FUSION
CHEFS ARE TAKING VIETNAMESE CUISINE TO ANOTHER LEVEL

© KEVIN LEE

Above: Small plates, Saigonita-style

STREET FOOD 101

Care to chomp down on some grilled corn doused in green onion oil or a steaming bowl of wonton noodle soup, washed down with an ice-cold glass of freshly squeezed sugar-cane and kumquat juice – all in the space of a few metres and for less than the price of a coffee back home? Welcome to Vietnam's glorious street-food scene.

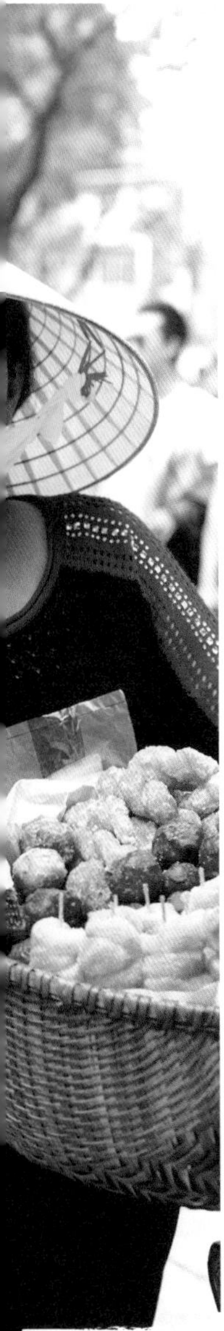

© Matt Munro / Lonely Planet

Above: Market sellers in Hanoi

STREET-FOOD CAPITAL OF THE WORLD

Vietnam is one of the world's best street-food destinations, offering the promise of bold and diverse flavours without ever stepping foot inside a restaurant. This is a place where you'll want to eat everything in sight, where you'll will yourself to get hungry just to be able to sample whatever deliciousness is being sold from that next cart, and where you'll have to weigh the value of a free but predictable hotel breakfast against the possibility of missing out on morning streetside delights.

The fantastic street-food scene has its origins in the longstanding Vietnamese tradition of living life out on the streets. Houses here tend to be narrow and cramped, especially in the cities: without the space to host groups of friends at home, the Vietnamese head outside, crowding around the pavement tables of the country's ubiquitous street-food stalls. There's a social nature to street-food joints, even for those eating alone – patrons are forced to sit close to each other, and the cook is just a few steps away preparing the food right in front of you.

Add to that the transitory nature of Vietnam's biggest cities, which draw people in from the countryside for work and study. These transient city-dwellers often live in rented rooms and houses, perhaps equipped only with the bare minimum – and a portable gas stove is better suited to late-night instant noodles than full meals. There's also another practical reason for the local love of street food: most homes are not air-conditioned, so it makes sense to avoid cooking in a hot kitchen on an even hotter day when you can simply let someone else do the work for just a little more outlay. And as the evenings cool down, a popular pastime is to simply hop on your motorbike and go for a drive, either alone or with friends, often with stops to snack, have a fruit shake or down a freshly brewed beer.

THE STREET-FOOD ECONOMY

Street-food stalls are a vital opportunity for the Vietnamese who run them. In this developing economy, where people are accustomed to creating jobs for themselves, selling street food is a great way to make some extra income. Setting up a street-food business requires very little start-up money, and the know-how to make just a single type of food, as well as the convenience of being able to set your own working hours – a perfect combination for those looking to top up the family income.

MUST-TRY STREET FOODS

While the street food of many countries leans toward snacks and quick bites, the unfussy nature of Vietnamese food means that entire meals can often be found on the sidewalk.

WHAT'S ON THE MENU?

Almost anything cooked up in restaurants can become street food here, but the list below focuses on dishes that are typically sold only on the streets.

BÁNH BAO

Steamed buns with a savoury filling, perhaps minced pork, onions, mushrooms and other vegetables. The slightly more expensive ones will have a hard-boiled chicken or quail egg inside. Just don't forget to remove the paper from the bottom before eating.

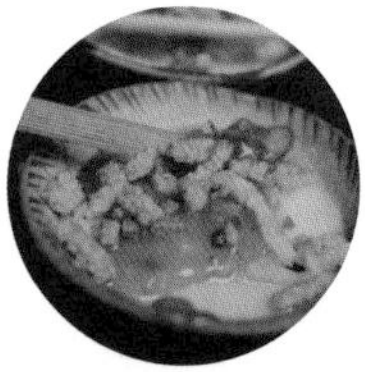

BÁNH BÈO

Small discs of steamed rice flour topped with dried shrimp, green onion oil and buttery croutons, with a fish sauce dressing. They're usually steamed at the vendor's home, then carried out by yoke to be sold.

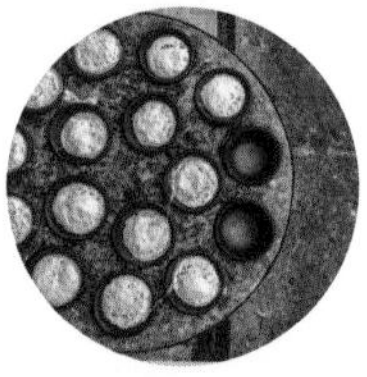

BÁNH CĂN

Mini rice-flour cakes cooked in tiny clay pots over an open fire, topped with minced pork, shrimp and a quail's egg. Often accompanied by shredded ripe mango and fish sauce.

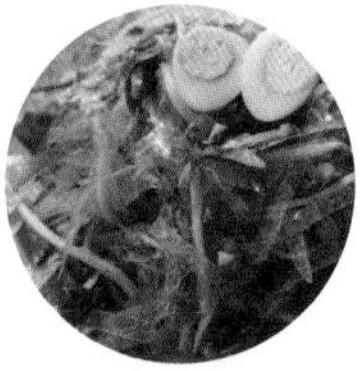

BÁNH TRÁNG TRỘN

Literally 'mixed rice paper', this student favourite is a plastic bag filled with a bewildering combination of flavours and textures: strips of dry rice paper, shredded green mango, hardboiled quail's eggs, tiny dried shrimp, fresh herbs, crispy shallots and roasted peanuts, tossed in a dressing of soy sauce, *sate* and kumquat, perhaps with a dollop of mayo.

HOW MUCH?

Street food like summer rolls are sold by the piece or by the amount. Vendors will often ask whether you want 15,000d or 20,000d worth; both equate to less than US$1, so if in doubt, just nod and let them go with the default.

BẮP XÀO

Kernels of sweet corn, wok-fried with butter, green onions and dried shrimp. Also look for its cousin, *bắp nướng*: grilled corn-on-the-cob slathered in green onion oil.

BÒ BÍA

Sweet or savoury rolls wrapped in spring-roll skins. Sweet fillings include fresh shredded coconut, crispy sugar crackers and sesame seeds, while the savoury version has cooked *jicama* (a potato-like tuber) and Chinese sausage, all dipped in a hoisin sauce.

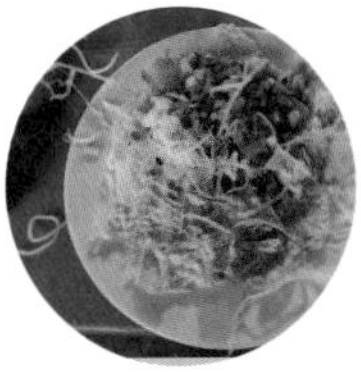

BỘT CHIÊN

Cubes of rice-flour cakes, crispy-fried on a large, circular griddle. When almost done, a beaten egg is poured over to bind everything together, then topped with chopped green onions and served on a bed of shredded green papaya with a tangy soy sauce-based dressing.

CHIM CÚT QUAY

Rotisserie quail, cooked up on a roadside grill and eaten with slices of cucumber and fresh herbs. Quails are small, so order a few and have them with a baguette for a filling meal.

GỎI ĐU ĐỦ

Shredded green papaya salad, topped with beef jerky or sliced pork and shrimp, plus roasted peanuts and crispy shrimp crackers, all doused with a fish-sauce-based dressing.

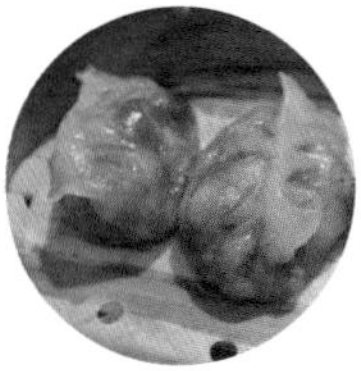

HÁ CẢO

Look for steamers filled with this delicious dim sum staple of dumplings stuffed with shrimp, pork or chives. Some places will also have them fried for a crispier texture, and they're often accompanied by a squirt of chilli sauce and some fresh herbs, plus a wooden skewer to eat with.

SÚP CUA

Slurp down a cup of this thick, delicious soup made from crab meat, eggs and shiitake mushrooms, finished off with a sprinkle of fresh coriander and a drizzle of sesame oil.

THỊT NƯỚNG ỐNG TRE

Most often found in the northern highlands, this is wild boar marinated in mountain herbs, stuffed inside a piece of bamboo and grilled. Slice open the bamboo and inhale the amazing cloud of steam before eating with sticky rice.

XÔI

Sweet or savoury sticky rice. Sweet versions are coloured with plant and fruit extracts (or food colouring), and eaten with shredded coconut or coconut milk. The savoury white version is often accompanied by peanuts, beans, sliced grilled chicken, or Chinese sausage.

EAT EVERYTHING REGRET NOTHING

As a developing country, Vietnam doesn't always enjoy the standards of hygiene that travellers may be used to. Many eateries are unlicensed, such as smaller street food stalls which are purposely designed to be packed up and moved at a moment's notice, and which have limited access to water, electricity and sanitation.

HOW TO EAT SAFELY

Food safety awareness is generally good in Vietnam, but the extent to which the chefs and servers who touch your food observe good practice obviously ranges enormously. Here are some ways to protect against food-related illness.

EAT WHERE AND WHEN OTHERS ARE EATING

Lots of customers usually means food is being turned over quickly, with less time to sit out and be exposed to contaminants. It also means that ingredients are being refreshed more often.

Above: Chefs cooking in an open kitchen setting

© Image Professionals GmbH / Alamy Stock Photo

BE OBSERVANT

Take a quick peek at the cooking area. Does the oil look clear and do the oil storage containers look clean? Is there some kind of netting to protect the food from flies, or is everything left out in the open? Does the food smell fresh? How careful is the vendor when switching between handling food, cleaning cloths and money? (Many vendors wear disposable gloves purely for convenience, and it's not uncommon to see someone use the same gloved hand to prepare food and to handle money.)

IS THE CUTLERY CLEAN?

Some restaurants wrap spoons and chopsticks in a paper sleeve to show they've been cleaned. In most places, however, they're placed in a container, usually uncovered, which will have been rummaged through by many hands in the course of a day. It's a good idea to give your utensils a quick clean by wiping them down with sanitiser, a napkin or a slice of the lime that's often found as a condiment on the table; alternatively, travel with your own reusables.

HYGIENE ON THE HOP

Making up a basic portable hygiene kit will help to keep your tummy in top shape during your travels. Include hand sanitiser (the spray kind is especially convenient) for when you can't wash your hands, a pack of wet wipes for cleaning surfaces or utensils, and something to deal with an upset stomach like activated charcoal or an anti-diarrhoeal. All these items are easily bought at any drug store or pharmacy in Vietnam.

SHOULD I EAT RAW FRUIT AND VEGETABLES?

The answer depends on how much you trust the vendor to have washed the produce. The rule of thumb for fruit is that anything with an inedible skin (watermelon, mango, banana) is usually fine; it's best to wash all other fruits thoroughly yourself before eating. Fresh herbs, sprouts and lettuce may retain traces of pesticides (or worse) if not washed properly; if eating soup, you can always ask for them to be dipped in boiling water before you load them into your bowl – ask for 'trụng' while pointing at the vegetables and making a dipping motion.

WHAT ABOUT THE ICE?

Ice used in urban areas is generally safe, especially if it's in evenly shaped cubes or cylinders, which indicate that it came from a factory (these typically use treated water). Oddly shaped shards of ice have been chipped from a larger block, and should be treated with caution or just avoided.

THE CULINARY CHECKLIST

Whether on a plate or in a cup, Vietnam's food and drink is so varied that the question of what to order can be overwhelming. Following the tips below should ensure that you don't miss any of the highlights.

Top eating and drinking experiences

© Iain Bagwell / Getty Images

BREAKFAST OF CHAMPIONS

Forgo the hotel breakfast in favour of phở – make a mission out of finding the best phở places near to where you're staying, try to discern the variations in the broths made by different chefs, and try out different meat combinations.

© Quynh Anh Nguyen / Getty Images

EAT REGIONALLY

Go for regional specialities whenever possible – like *cao lầu* noodles in Hoi An and *bún chả* in Hanoi – as you may not get a chance later. Many dishes aren't often available outside of the area that they originate in.

© AsianDream / Getty Images

CALL IN AN EXPERT

If you're not an adventurous eater, signing up for a street food tour early on in your trip might serve to demystify eating in Vietnam, and give you a taste of what you might like to try more of independently.

CAFFEINATE LOCAL-STYLE

Skip the streetside carts where the coffee comes ready-brewed, as it's often made with artificial syrup. Instead, go for one serving Vietnamese 'drip coffee', where the grounds are placed in a metal cup-top filter, allowing the brew to trickle slowly through. The Vietnamese are also masters at unusual coffee innovations, adding everything from raw whipped egg to yoghurt and coconut. Trying as many variations as you can is a fun way to explore this rich coffee culture.

© NiceProspects-Prime / Alamy Stock Photo

THE FRENCH CONNECTION

Vietnam can be a great place for a quality French meal that won't break the bank. Top spots include Jardin Des Sens in Ho Chi Minh City, owned by the Michelin-starred Pourcel brothers, and Hanoi's Press Club, overseen by Michelin-starred chef Alain Dutournier.

PARKLIFE

Vietnam's parks are great places to sample street snacks in a social atmosphere. Grab a bench in the late afternoon or on a weekend and delve into whatever snack comes by on a yoke or cart; before long, you'll probably be engaged in a chat with locals eager to practise their English.

© Greg Elms / Lonely Planet

ASK THE LOCALS

Instead of simply asking for restaurant recommendations (which tend to yield tourist-centric answers), try asking local people where they like to eat; you may well end up in a tucked-away streetside place where you'll be elbow-to-elbow with locals, smothered in a cloud of meaty smoke and enjoying some classic Vietnamese food.

STAPLES & SPECIALITIES

© Cao Anh Tuan / 500px

Left: Tending to the rice fields in Hoa Binh province

Nearly two-thirds of Vietnam's population lives in rural areas, and the hearts of most city-dwellers remain firmly planted in the countryside, with its endless fields of rice, tropical fruit waiting to be picked from the trees and ponds teeming with fish. The degree of separation between most Vietnamese and the provenance of the food they eat is much smaller than in many other countries; this is a place where the ingredients of lunch or dinner may well come directly from parents, grandparents or wider family.

While times are certainly changing, the Vietnamese have proven somewhat resistant to fast food and processed products – meals here still revolve around healthy, whole foods. Rice in its myriad forms is the base for practically every dish, from breakfast to dessert. With a lengthy coastline and a labyrinth of waterways, ponds and streams, it's no surprise that fresh fish and shrimp, combined with fermented fish sauce, make up nearly 14% of the total average consumption of fish and meat, followed by pork and then ever-smaller degrees of chicken, duck and beef.

Fruits and vegetables also play a starring role in Vietnamese food culture. Vegetables in one form or another feature in most meals, from the raw sprouts thrown into a breakfast-time bowl of noodle soup to the ubiquitous condiments based around pickled onions, greens and radishes. Fruit is eaten as a between-meals snack or a dessert, and incorporated into salads of banana bud, pomelo and green papaya.

Finally, herbs and aromatics are the soul of Vietnamese cooking. Ginger, garlic, shallots and a smorgasbord of strange-sounding fresh herbs help meals to achieve balance without being overly bold or spicy.

RICE

Many national cuisines bounce between corn, rice and wheat, but in Vietnam it's all rice, all the time. The phrase for having a meal – *ăn cơm* – literally translates as 'eating rice', and the average Vietnamese gets through 150kg (330lb) of the stuff per year.

© Sasin Tipchai / 500px

Above: Family time amid the rice paddies

RICE IS LIFE

For the Vietnamese, a meal without rice is no meal at all. Over thousands of years, much of the country's culture and history has been built around rice, from growing, processing and transporting it to selling, cooking and eating it – so it's no

A LOW-ON-CASH CROP

It's estimated that an average farming household cultivating a 1-acre (0.4 hectare) plot of rice makes an annual profit of just US$220 per year, after deducting the expense of seedlings, harvesting and animal feed – quite a startling difference to Vietnam's average annual household income of US$2200.

wonder that it has permeated almost every facet of life, from folk proverbs and religious beliefs to everyday customs.

FROM FIELD TO MARKET

Vietnam's main rice-producing regions are the north's Red River Delta, serving the domestic market and responsible for 18% of the country's yield; south of Ho Chi Minh City, the Mekong Delta produces 52% of Vietnam's rice. Both areas mainly employ wet rice cultivation, a laborious process that takes 3–4 months from start to finish, including ploughing the field, germinating seedlings and then replanting them in the main fields, plus fertilising, weeding, watering and harvesting, much of it done without machinery (ploughs are often still pulled by buffalo). Processing rice involves bashing the plants to remove the grains, drying the kernels in the sun, threshing to separate edible grains from husks, milling to remove the bran, and finally polishing and sorting.

As one of the world's leading exporters, Vietnam grows about 200 types of rice, and in 2019 an organic, long-grain jasmine variety from Soc Trang in the Mekong Delta was crowned the World's Best Rice by *Rice Trader* magazine. At the market, however, rice stalls usually display about 20 or so buckets, each marked with the variety – plain, glutinous (sticky), broken, brown and so forth – and often the province where the rice was grown (or its country of origin in the case of imported rice, usually Thailand or Japan).

BUYING RICE

Many Vietnamese develop a personal relationship with the market trader who sells them their rice, getting advice on which variety suits individual preferences, and which has been newly harvested (this is when rice is at its sweetest and most aromatic). Savvy shoppers will know to look for grains that are shiny but not too white (as this could indicate rice has been overly polished or treated with chemicals) and even-sized, without broken or discoloured pieces.

NOWHERE IS AS BEAUTIFUL AS OUR VIETNAM WITH HER ENDLESS SEAS OF RICE FIELDS

TRADITIONAL VIETNAMESE POEM

RICE BLESSINGS

In the north, it's customary for adults to say 'cơm muối' ('rice and salt') every time a child sneezes – these two items are common altar offerings made to guard against evil spirits.

THE STORY OF BROKEN RICE

If you had to eat just one dish for the rest of your life, you could do a lot worse than Vietnam's classic *cơm tấm*, broken rice slathered with a multitude of tasty toppings.

A HUMBLE DISH TRANSFORMED

Found everywhere in southern Vietnam, the classic one-plate meal of *cơm tấm* got its start as a peasant dish, made using broken grains unfit for market and typically reserved as chicken feed or eaten by poor rice farmers themselves. However, as the farmers moved to the city, they introduced *cơm tấm* to the residents of today's Ho Chi Minh City (then Saigon), who promptly dressed it up with nicer cuts of meat and a bevy of add-ons.

It's said that the secret behind *cơm tấm's* addictive nature is its broken grains, which enable a better coating of the fish sauce-based dressing and increase the flavour. Today, *cơm tấm* is one of the most popular breakfast dishes in Ho Chi Minh City – so much so that, somewhat ironically, rice has to be purposely broken to meet the demand.

While there are entire restaurants dedicated to all the different variations of this one dish, you'll also find *cơm tấm* sold on the street, especially in southern Vietnam. Follow your nose to the delicious smell of grilled meat with notes of honey and lemongrass. As it's traditionally a breakfast item, don't be shocked if you arrive at 9am and find your neighbourhood stall has sold out. But these days, *cơm tấm* can usually be found throughout the day, too, with street food sellers also popping up in the evenings to serve the late night crowd.

CƠM TẤM TOPPINGS

As a default, *cơm tấm* usually comes with a char-grilled pork chop (*sườn*), but there is also a handful of possible additions: steamed egg quiche with minced pork, wood-ear mushrooms and bean thread (*chả trứng*); grilled pork belly (*ba rọi*); short ribs (*sườn non*); grilled pork sausage (*nem nướng*); grilled chicken (*gà nướng*); shredded pork skin tossed with roasted rice powder (*bì*); or a fried egg (*trứng chiên*). The whole plate is topped with green onion oil, a few slices of cucumber and tomato, plus pickled carrots and white radish, and a thick, sweet, glossy fish-sauce-based dressing is drizzled over the whole dish. Most places will also serve a little bowl of broth alongside it, too.

© James Pham

Above: *Cơm tấm* has risen from make-do staple to culinary classic

HAVING IT ALL

While you can have cơm tấm *topped with any of the toppings displayed at stalls, it's a safe bet to just say 'đầy đủ' (meaning 'everything') with a flourish of the hand – the result will be a true breakfast of champions.*

RICE PORRIDGE

Known as *cháo* or *congee*, carb-heavy rice porridge is a classic comfort food and serves as the perfect foil to some of Vietnam's more pungent specialities.

CONGEE FOR THE SOUL

For most Vietnamese, *cháo* is the ultimate comfort food, as hallowed as chicken noodle soup is to Americans. A simple porridge, it's made with regular rice or a mix of regular and glutinous rice, to which extra water is added depending upon whether a loose or thick consistency is required; the rice can also be dry-roasted before cooking to impart a smoky flavour.

Easily digestible, *cháo* is served to babies transitioning to solid foods, and is a staple when recovering from illness or surgery and for the elderly. Eating a piping hot bowl of *cháo* makes you sweat, so it's also viewed as detoxifying, making it popular when feeling unwell, when hungover (which is why you'll sometimes see street stalls selling it until the wee morning hours) and as a warming breakfast on winter mornings.

Takeaways sell plain *cháo* topped with anything from seafood, minced beef or fish to pea purée, eel and cheese. Its relatively bland taste makes *cháo* the perfect vehicle to deliver bold flavours. Salty pairings include salted duck eggs and fish-sauce-slathered, shell-on shrimp or scrambled eggs; pickled radishes and mustard greens add crunch and sourness. There are even sweet versions of *cháo*, flavoured with pandan leaves, black sesame seeds and the date-like jujube fruit.

Below: A steaming bowl of *cháo* is ideal comfort food

© Phongthon Preuksrirat / Shutterstock

WHERE TO GET YOUR CHÁO FIX

Aside from plain cháo*, popular variations include a Singaporean-style version with frog braised in soy sauce, plus* cháo *cooked with squid or with offal (including heart, liver and intestines). More commonly, though, you'll find* cháo *wherever boiled chicken dishes are sold (usually things like sliced chicken with rice, chicken and cabbage salad, or chicken soup with glass noodles); cooked in chicken stock laced with slivers of fresh ginger, the* cháo *will be packed with flavour, and is served with deep-fried breadsticks for a lovely texture contrast.*

Rice-based products

The Vietnamese make a host of food products from the humble rice grain; the list below includes some of the most common.

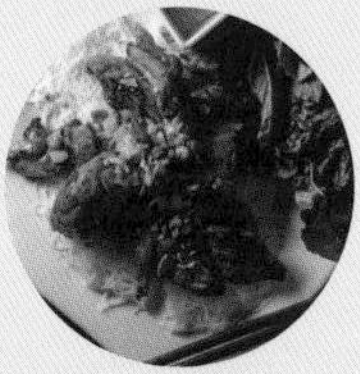

BÁNH HỚI

The thinnest of rice noodles, steamed as an accompaniment to roast or boiled pork and grilled shrimp.

BÚN

Rice-flour vermicelli noodles, incorporated into hot soups or eaten at room temperature with grilled pork.

HỦ TIẾU

Translucent and slightly chewy tapioca and rice flour noodles, used in Chinese- and Khmer-style soups.

TRÀ GẠO LỨC

Brown-rice tea, made with roasted rice which gives it a deliciously smoky flavour.

BÁNH TRÁNG

Rice paper is made by pouring a thin rice-flour batter over a piece of cloth stretched over a steamer; the delicate sheets are then dried on woven bamboo mats, which impart a cross-hatched pattern.

BÁNH PHỞ

The flat rice noodles that are an integral part of Vietnam's favourite noodle soup are made in the same way as rice paper, though the thicker sheets are cut into strips before being dried.

THÍNH

Made from grinding roasted grains of rice, this roasted rice powder gives an earthy, smoky flavour to pork sausages, spit-roasted veal and shredded pork skin; it also adds a pleasing grittiness to the latter.

RƯỢU GẠO

Rice wine, made with regular or glutinous rice, fermented with water and yeast and distilled. There are black and brown-rice variations; medicinal wine is infused with herbs, roots and even whole animals.

SPRING ROLLS

Created as a means of celebrating long-awaited spring vegetables, Vietnam's spring rolls are smaller, lighter and don't include the cabbage, water chestnuts, bamboo shoots or roast pork of the Chinese version.

© imageBROKER / Alamy Stock Photo

Left: Labour-intensive spring rolls are a popular street food **Opposite:** Fried spring rolls alongside their fresh counterpart, *gỏi cuốn*

THE ELEMENTS OF A SPRING ROLL

While spring rolls go by different names around Vietnam – *chả giò* in the south, *chả ram* or *chả cuốn* in central Vietnam, *nem rán* in the north – they're basically the same wherever you go: a filling of minced pork, carrots, wood-ear mushrooms and glass noodles that's bound together with egg, wrapped in a thin skin, then deep-fried. Three types of wrappers are used: regular rice paper, recognisable by its uneven, bubbly texture when fried; *bánh tráng rế*, a woven, almost lace-like wrapper made with rice and mung beans, which originated in the Mekong Delta town of Can Tho; or the wheat-based Chinese-style skins that are griddle-cooked and sold fresh in markets.

IT'S ALL IN THE NAME

Northern Vietnamese scratch their heads as to why spring rolls are known as chả giò *in the south, given* chả *is typically a fried minced-meat patty and* giò *a ham-like cold cut made with seasoned, steamed minced meat.*

REGIONAL ROLLS

Fillings vary by region, and even by household. In the north, you might find bean sprouts, shredded kohlrabi, meaty mushrooms and even snails in the mix, while the southern iteration can incorporate shredded tubers like taro or the potato-like *jicama* for extra substance. Distinct regional variations include *nem cua bể* from Haiphong on Vietnam's northeastern coast, stuffed with shrimp and crab and wrapped in a distinctive square shape; *chả dông*, made from lizard meat tempered with lemongrass, a speciality of Phu Yen province on the south-central coast; and *chả ram tôm đất* from Binh Dinh, which sometimes includes a whole freshwater shrimp with the tail sticking out of one end for effect.

A REFINED ART

While spring rolls feature on the menu of practically every Vietnamese restaurant outside of Vietnam, they're not as common as one might think in the country itself. The labour-intensive filling requires lots of soaking, peeling, chopping and mixing, while wrapping the spring rolls is an art in itself. The rice paper has to be moistened to make it pliable enough to use; get it too wet, and it'll disintegrate, too dry and it'll crack. Wrap the rolls too loosely and they'll burst in the hot oil; squeeze them too tight and the outside will burn before the inside is cooked. If the filling has too much egg or other liquid, it'll cause the oil to splash everywhere on contact; too dry and the spring roll comes apart when eaten.

The best place to buy spring rolls in Vietnam (other than in supermarket frozen sections, which often have a dozen or so varieties) are streetside stalls selling grilled pork noodle dishes (these are *bún thịt nướng* in the south and *bún chả* in the north); they're also a popular food during Lunar New Year and other feast occasions.

© leekhoailang / Getty Images

Above: Producing perfect spring rolls is a delicate art

EAT SPRING ROLLS LIKE A PRO

To eat spring rolls when they're served on their own, use a lettuce leaf as a wrapper, pile on some of the accompanying vermicelli rice noodles, herbs and sprouts, then dip the whole thing into the fish-sauce-based nước chấm *dressing. This can get messy, so an alternative is to put everything together in a bowl and just drizzle the* nước chấm *over the top.*

STARCHES

While rice rules the roost, Vietnamese cooking does make use of several other starches, the most common of which are listed below.

BEANS

From mung and soy, black to adzuki, beans are incorporated into savoury stews, made into blocks of tofu and, when mashed and sweetened, used in desserts.

CASSAVA

Boiled cassava with a bit of salt was a traditional hard-times staple. Shredded, it lends a crunchiness to stir-fries, and is made into grilled or steamed cassava cakes with coconut milk and a pinch of salt.

CORN

Grilled on the cob then dipped in green onion oil, eaten as kernels fried with butter and dried shrimp as a street-food snack, and incorporated into sweet puddings; it's also made into 'corn milk', a blend of ground corn, cow's milk, condensed milk and sugar.

GLUTINOUS RICE FLOUR

The base for many chewy Vietnamese snacks including the thick round discs known as *bánh giầy* (often eaten with steamed pork sausage), as well as a host of sweet and savoury cakes, which are steamed in banana leaves and stuffed with coconut, or with pork and shrimp.

TAPIOCA

Cassava starch is made into tiny translucent tapioca pearls to use in sweet soups and bubble tea, while tapioca flour is used in cakes, as a thickening agent, and is mixed with rice flour to make noodles.

TUBERS

Vietnamese cooking uses a host of different tubers, though rarely on their own in the way of mashed potatoes or French fries. Instead, colourful tubers like taro, purplish yams, orange sweet potatoes and (less commonly) white potatoes are found in savoury soups, stews and stir-fries, as well as sweet desserts.

WHEAT FLOUR

The basis for crunchy baguettes; breadcrumbs are occasionally used as a coating for deep-fried dishes.

Opposite, from top: Fish sauce, in production and table-ready

FISH SAUCE

If there's one ingredient that sets Vietnamese cuisine apart from other Southeast Asian cooking styles, it is pungent *nước mắm*, an essential element of almost all the country's specialities.

THE FUNDAMENTALS OF FISH SAUCE

Vietnamese *nước mắm* is made from fermented fish, usually anchovies or mackerel, which are packed in sea salt into big wooden vats or large earthenware jars and left for at least eight months. Natural bacteria breaks down the flesh, leaving a thick slurry from which the amber liquid is strained.

Nước mắm is made all along Vietnam's coast, but some of the best is produced on Phu Quoc island in the Gulf of Thailand, and in the coastal town of Phan Thiet, northeast of Ho Chi Minh City; both are lauded for their prime marine terroir.

Additional flavours like pineapple, sugar or honey are sometimes added to *nước mắm* (especially if it's made at home), but traditionally it only contains fish and salt, with no additives or preservatives. It's also graded in the same manner as olive oil: premium *nước mắm*, with higher concentrations of nitrogen indicating more intensity, comes from the first draining. Other signs of a high-quality sauce are a light amber colour, a clear taste of fish, and a good balance of salt and sweet.

The soul of Vietnamese cooking, fish sauce finds its way into almost every savoury dish – as a marinade for meats, to add umami in place

MẮM

Made in much the same way as fish sauce, mắm *is fish packed in salt and left to ferment for about two months, leaving the flesh intact. Go to any Mekong Delta market and you'll find still-moist fish and shrimp* mắm *piled high, ready to be used in broths, hot pots and as a dip for raw or boiled vegetables.*

© Tran Qui Thinh / Shutterstock

of salt, as a pickling agent, or as the backbone of dishes like crispy fish-sauce-glazed chicken wings. In some Vietnamese homes, *nước mắm* is served straight out of the bottle as a very salty dipping sauce, but it's more commonly diluted into *nước chấm* (mixed with sugar, minced garlic and shallots, chillies and some type of acid like lime juice or vinegar). A similar recipe is used for the fish-sauce-based dressings poured over broken rice and cold noodle dishes.

© Image Professionals GmbH / Alamy Stock Photo

ANYONE FOR ICE-CREAM?

Fancy fish sauce in a dessert? Ralf's Gelato in Ho Chi Minh City churns out Italian-style gelato incorporating nước mắm *– but instead of tasting fishy, this wonderfully smooth artisanal ice-cream has the same kind of appeal of salted caramel, with just a hint of fish-sauce goodness.*

SPICES AND SEASONINGS

From sweet to spicy, bitter to sour, Vietnamese cooking is underpinned by an abundance of flavour-bomb seasonings.

COMMON FLAVOURS

The ingredients below provide the five fall-back flavourings of Vietnamese cuisine:

Aromatics

Herbs; and onions, shallots and garlic, often crispy fried and added as a garnish.

Bitter

Peel from limes and mandarin oranges.

Sour

Fruits like lime, kumquat, pineapple, tamarind or star fruit; vinegar (sometimes fruit or fermented rice varieties).

Spicy

Green and red bird's eye chillies, pepper, ginger, lemongrass, *sate* sauce.

Sweet

Honey; sugar (white, brown, palm, rock, cane and coconut) is caramelised to give a beautiful brown colour to several dishes.

MSG

Known as mì chính *in the north,* bột ngọt *in the south, MSG is used liberally in Vietnamese cuisine to add a punch of flavour. In restaurants and soup stalls where they assemble your bowl to order, you can say 'không để mì chính (bột ngọt)' if you don't want MSG in your food, but at ready-made meals places and most street food joints, it's probably cooked into the dish already.*

SEASONING SPECIFICS

The use of spices and seasonings differs from region to region. Northerners tend to prefer their food on the bland side (especially with phở and other noodle dishes), while the the sultry climate of central Vietnam encourages bolder, spicier flavours, and the perpetual summer of the south invites sweeter, fattier food, with just a hint of heat.Common seasoning ingredients include:

COCONUT

The water from fresh green nuts adds sweetness to steamed and braised dishes; coconut milk (made by soaking and squeezing the grated flesh) adds richness to curries, stews and, if sweetened, to desserts.

CINNAMON

The bark flavours phở broth, and the powder is used as a meat marinade and in desserts.

FIVE-SPICE POWDER

Used to marinate meats and flavour stews and grilled dishes, comprising cinnamon, cloves, fennel, star anise and Sichuan peppercorns; the Vietnamese version can also include coriander seeds, the ginger-like *thảo quả*, annatto (which adds a red colour) and mandarin orange zest.

GALANGAL

Similar to ginger but with more astringent zing, galangal is sliced fresh into stir-fries and braised dishes, used to marinate meat and to add flavour to steamed seafood.

GINGER

Fresh ginger finds its way into braised meat dishes, especially fish and chicken, is candied with sugar as a snack, made into sweet syrups to accompany silken tofu, and steeped as a tea.

OYSTER SAUCE

Thick and brown, made from oysters, salt, sugar and corn starch, this versatile sauce is used to marinate meats and is added to stir-fries and dipping sauces.

SESAME

White or black sesame seeds are used to flavour dipping sauces and marinades or to sprinkle as a garnish. Toasted sesame oil adds a wonderful fragrance to marinades and stir-fries.

STAR ANISE

Dried star anise adds flavour to phở broth, curries and stews, and compliments stronger-tasting meats like oxtail, duck and intestines.

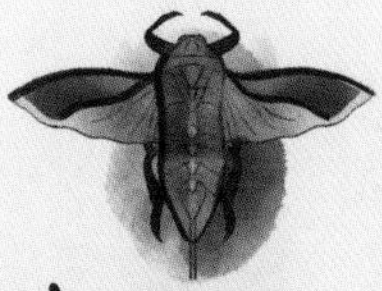

CÀ CUỐNG

A pheromone extracted from male giant water bugs (lethocerus indicus), this aromatic oil features in northern Vietnamese dishes. Just a couple of drops add an intoxicating floral note to steamed-rice rolls, noodle soups and pan-fried fish with turmeric. Unsurprisingly, cà cuống *is very expensive; synthetic essences are more common than the real deal.*

TURMERIC

Fresh or powdered turmeric gives a beautiful golden colour to dishes like savoury *bánh xèo* crepes, yellow *mì quảng* noodles and the Hanoi grilled-fish dish of *chả cá lã vọng*.

MIX IT UP

In addition to selling individual spices, spice vendors often have their own homemade mixes for curries, stews and ragouts which make easy work of recreating Vietnamese flavours once back in your home country.

Dip in!

Vietnamese cuisine is built around intense tastes, and in addition to the multiple seasonings added to food before and during cooking, table sauces and dips add a final layer of flavour.

© Makidotvn / Getty Images

Common dips

AGED BEAN CURD

(chao)

Likened by some to blue cheese for its strong flavour and chunky texture, *chao* adds umami to vegetarian and duck dishes, and is diluted with garlic, chilli and sugar as a dipping sauce for boiled vegetables and goat dishes. It's also eaten just with rice.

CARAMELISED FISH SAUCE

(kho quẹt)

Originally a hardship staple, this thick, syrupy sauce is made from pork fat, dried shrimp, shallots, garlic and other spices cooked down with fish sauce; it's used as a dip for boiled okra, cauliflower and melon.

FERMENTED FISH PASTE

(mắm nêm)

Incredibly pungent, this sauce is made from salted and fermented fish, roasted rice powder, pineapple, garlic, chilli and sugar. It often accompanies fresh summer rolls and other dishes that use rice noodles or rice paper.

FERMENTED SHRIMP PASTE

(mắm ruốc)

Darker brown in colour and not as 'fishy' tasting as its cousin *mắm tôm, mắm ruốc* is fermented for much longer and is used in cooking as well as for dipping sour fruits like green mango and guava.

FERMENTED SHRIMP PASTE

(mắm tôm)

Notable for its distinctive dark-purplish colour and very strong aroma, fermented shrimp paste is the most pungent of all the sauces. A tiny dollop goes a long way in adding umami to noodle soups; it's also diluted with sugar and a squeeze of kumquat as a dip for crispy fried tofu and boiled pork with pickled baby aubergine.

FISH SAUCE

(nước mắm)

Pungent and strong-tasting, straight fish sauce is used for dipping bland food like boiled vegetables or meats; it's more commonly diluted into *nước chấm* which, in addition to the usual lime, sugar, minced garlic and chillies, can also have added fresh ginger to accompany chicken and duck dishes, and shredded mango to pair with fish. In Central Vietnam, tamarind fish sauce is served with eel and fish dishes.

HOISIN SAUCE

(tương đen)

This dark sauce of fermented soybeans is used as a condiment for phở or diluted much like a *nước chấm* to dip fresh summer rolls, roasted veal and grilled pork sausages.

SALT AND CHILLI

(muối ớt)

A simple dip for curried and grilled meats, also used to bring out the sweetness in fruit.

SALT, PEPPER AND LIME JUICE

(muối tiêu chanh)

The default sauce used to bring out the delicate flavours of seafood and boiled chicken. Another variation adds green chillies, lime leaves and condensed milk.

SOY SAUCE

(xì dầu)

Used straight from the bottle with some chopped chilli, soy sauce is often paired with vegetarian dishes, fried rice and Chinese-style meats like crispy pork belly and roasted duck.

© Kyoko Uchida / Alamy Stock Photo

Opposite & above: Hoisin sauce and *nước chấm* dipping sauce

SRIRACHA

In most restaurants and street stalls, you'll see a bottle of the thick red chilli sauce known here as tương ớt. *The well-loved Huy Fong sriracha that graces restaurant tables the world over, with its rooster logo and bright red colour, originates from a recipe devised by Vietnamese-American David Tran – but you'll rarely, if ever, encounter his brand in Vietnam due to its comparatively high cost as an import; it also has a more sour taste than the chilli sauce commonly used in Vietnam*

Right: Fresh herbs and greens are a market staple in Vietnam
Below: Thai basil

© Emmanuel Chansarel-Bourigon / Getty Images

© RomanBabakin / Getty Images

HERBS

Fresh herbs are an integral part of Vietnamese cuisine, served raw with everything from soups to rolls or salads, and cooked into food to add a delicious depth.

COMMONLY USED HERBS

CORIANDER

(rau mùi in the north, ngò rí in the south)

So widely used that a free bunch is automatically added to vegetables bought at markets. Chopped stems and leaves are added to soups, salads and bánh mì sandwiches.

DILL

(thìa là)

More commonly used in northern Vietnam, dill is deployed to reduce overly fishy notes in fish soups, fishcakes and pan-fried fish with turmeric and peanuts.

FISH MINT

(diếp cá)

People either love or hate these smooth, heart-shaped leaves with a strong fishy taste that accompany summer rolls, savoury crepes and salads.

MINT

(bạc hà)

A refreshing addition to salads, also used as a garnish.

PERILLA

(tía tô)

Also known as shiso, these distinctly purple leaves with an earthy taste are paired with noodle soups and frog, snail or eel dishes.

PIPER LOLOT

(lá lốt)

Often mistranslated as betel leaf, these fragrant, almost waxy leaves are commonly wrapped around minced beef before grilling.

RICE-PADDY HERB

(rau ngổ in the north, ngò ôm in the south)

Reminiscent of cumin, but with a slightly bitter aftertaste, rice-paddy herb is often eaten with phở and *canh chua* (sweet and sour soup).

SAWTOOTH CORIANDER

(ngò gai)

Don't be afraid of these long leaves with prickly (and entirely edible) edges: the strong flavour goes well with bamboo dishes and with phở.

BASIL

(húng quế)

Very common, and used cooked and raw, Thai basil (distinguishable by its purplish stem) is always included with the fresh herbs that accompany phở, steamed rice rolls and cold noodles.

VIETNAMESE BALM

(kinh giới)

These large, lemony flavoured leaves accompany noodle soups as well as fried tofu with fermented shrimp paste.

VIETNAMESE MINT

(rau râm)

The strong, peppery taste pairs well with duck embryos and chicken-cabbage salad, and imparts a lovely flavour to steamed seafood.

HERB HABITS

When eating fresh herbs, pluck the leaves from the fibrous stems and tear into bite-sized pieces; and at the same time, give the herbs a quick look to make sure they've been washed well and are free of dirt or insects.

FRUIT

With its diverse terrain and tropical climate, Vietnam cultivates a huge range of seriously delicious fruit. As well as exotic varieties, look out for twists on familiar fruits, from finger-sized bananas to sweet-fleshed mandarin oranges with a dark green skin.

VIETNAMESE FRUITS

As well as being eaten for dessert, fruit finds its way into Vietnamese savoury dishes – pineapple is used in stir-fries and soups, while pomelo or unripe mango and papaya are the star of refreshing salads. The following are some of Vietnam's most common fruits.

COCONUT

(dừa)

There's nothing quite as refreshing as a chilled coconut water, drunk from the nut on a hot day. Watch as the seller deftly lops off the top, leaving a slit for your straw; when you're done, spoon out the sweet, jelly-like flesh for a tasty snack.

DRAGON FRUIT

(thanh long)

Dragon fruit is easily identifiable by its raucously fuchsia skin and wispy green tendrils. Peel the skin and bite into the lightly sweet white or pink flesh; the seeds are edible.

DURIAN

(sầu riêng)

The dangerously spiky exterior shouts 'don't eat me!', but the Vietnamese love this creamy yellow fruit. It's known for its offensive odour, often compared to sweaty socks and onions – don't even think of bringing one into your hotel room or on to a plane, as they're often banned.

GUAVA

(ổi)

Green with white or pink flesh, guavas can be washed and eaten with the skin on. Chilli salt brings out the slightly sweet flavour.

© hadynyah / Getty Images

Above: Fruit galore at a Mekong Delta floating market

EASY-ACCESS FRUIT

To enjoy fruit without having to peel and cut it yourself (especially convenient during hotel stays), look for pre-cut fruit packages in supermarkets, which often come with a bag of chilli salt conveniently included. Most of the fruits sold this way will have been peeled first, and hygiene standards are generally good, though use your judgement before buying.

JACKFRUIT

(mít)

A rough exterior belies the yellow, crunchy segments inside, with a sweet, almost bubblegum-like taste and big inedible seeds.

LONGAN

(nhãn)

Peel the thin, brittle skin and feast on sweet, translucent flesh surrounding a single inedible seed.

LYCHEE

(vải)

Bigger and juicier than a longan – peel the thin, reddish skin to reveal a soft white flesh around an inedible seed.

MANGO

(xoài)

Dozens of mango varieties are grown in Vietnam. Sweet mangoes are typically soft and yellow, while hard green mangoes are often quite sour, eaten with chilli salt or a savoury fermented fish paste.

MANGOSTEEN

(măng cụt)
Twist open the purplish rind of this mandarin-sized fruit to find the fleshy, tangy-sweet white segments inside.

PASSION FRUIT

(chanh leo)
A favourite of hotel breakfasts, with soft, yellowish-orange flesh, crunchy, edible seeds and a pleasant sweet-and-tart taste.

POMELO

(bưởi)
With the look and taste of a super-sized grapefruit, the pomelo's juicy, kernel-like fruit can be yellowish-green or pink.

RAMBUTAN

(chôm chôm)
Red with coarse, greenish hair; twist open the hard exterior to reveal the pearly white fruit - sweet with a hint of tartness.

ROSE APPLE

(roi in the north, mận in the south)
Light and airy, these crimson fruits are shaped like a knobbly pear; wash well, then eat the perfumed, firm flesh with the skin on.

SOURSOP

(mãng cầu)
With a dark green, prickly exterior and an intensely sweet-and-tart, citrusy flesh, soursop is a popular flavour for fruit shakes.

STAR APPLE

(vú sữa)
A purplish green fruit with a smooth, shiny skin and fragrantly sweet flesh; the juice is sticky and milky, so cut them open and eat with a spoon.

STAR FRUIT

(khế)
Sweet, sour and citrusy, the star fruit can be washed and eaten with the skin on. They're also used in soups and rice-paper rolls.

SHADES OF CITRUS

Green limes are available everywhere in Vietnam, but lemons are a rarity here, usually found only in speciality shops.

© Nga Nguyen / Getty Images

Above: Fresh produce stall, Hanoi

VEGETABLES

Vietnamese food is known for being fresh and light thanks, in part, to its liberal use of vegetables. Leafy greens are often eaten raw or in a soup, while other vegetables are stir-fried or used in soups and stews, or pickled into table-top condiments.

VIETNAMESE VEGGIES

While plenty of vegetables familiar to international visitors – carrots, cauliflower, tomatoes, cucumbers – are grown in Vietnam, there are a few which might not be so easily identifiable:

AMARANTH

(rau dền)

A leafy green distinguishable by its small green leaves with a reddish centre. Commonly used in simple soups flavoured with minced pork, or boiled and dipped in a salty sauce like *nước mắm*.

© Johnny Jones / Alamy Stock Photo

Above: A field of greens near Hoi An

SALADS

*While plain sliced tomatoes and cucumbers often accompany rice dishes, mixed salads of lettuce and other raw veg in a vinaigrette-type dressing are practically unheard of in Vietnamese homes. Instead, local-style salads (*gỏi *or* nộm*) are heartier, leaning towards julienned mango, lotus stems and banana bud (the flower of the banana tree) topped with sliced pork or shrimp, and tossed with a fish-sauce-based dressing.*

BAMBOO SHOOTS

(măng)

Young shoots are used in soups and stews and pickled as a condiment.

BITTER MELON

(khổ qua)

Almost inedibly bitter on first try, this bumpy-skinned specimen has a way of growing on you, especially when it's stuffed with minced pork and wood-ear mushrooms in a clear soup broth, or sliced and cooked with scrambled eggs.

CHAYOTE

(su su)

Belonging to the gourd family, *su su* is used much like *su hào* (kohlrabi) as its crunchy texture stands up well in soups and stir-fries. It's often sold pre-julienned in supermarkets.

JAPANESE/THAI EGGPLANT

(cà tím/cà pháo)

Long, thin and purple, *cà tím* are usually grilled until soft and topped with green onion oil and minced pork. Smaller, rounder and slightly bitter *cà pháo* are typically pickled and eaten as an accompaniment to soups.

JAPANESE PUMPKIN

(bí đỏ)

These green-skinned, orange-fleshed pumpkins are commonly found in soups, dressed up with some minced pork and green onions. The seeds are toasted shell-on as a snack.

KOHLRABI

(su hào)

A knobbly, pale-green brassica with a mildly sweet taste sometimes likened to broccoli stem; it retains a lovely, crispy consistency in stir-fries and soups.

MALABAR SPINACH

(rau mồng tơi)

Another leafy green, often found in Vietnamese soups. Its heart-shaped leaves are said to be a natural coolant and are also used to treat insomnia, wounds and to prevent weak bones.

MORNING GLORY/WATER SPINACH

(rau muống)

Grown practically anywhere there's fresh water, *rau muống* is extremely common and cheap. The crunchy stems are shredded and eaten raw with noodle soups, while leaves and stems are stir-fried with garlic as a side dish.

© Radius Images / Alamy Stock Photo

Above: Sorting the stock at Ben Thanh market, Ho Chi Minh City

PEPPER ELDER

(rau càng cua)

This fast-growing plant with small, heart-shaped leaves and a fresh but slightly bitter taste is often mixed with boiled chicken and dressed with a vinaigrette. It's also used to treat skin disorders and rheumatic joint pain.

WINGED BEAN

(đậu rồng)

'Dragon bean' in Vietnamese, these mild-tasting pulses resemble the body of a dragon; they're often paired with salty sauces like fermented or caramelised fish, or stir-fried with meat.

COOL-CLIMATE FRUITS AND VEGETABLES

It may come as a surprise to see fruit and vegetables not typically associated with tropical climates in Vietnam's markets. Artichokes, strawberries, asparagus and broccoli were introduced by the French, planted in the moderately cool Dalat highlands where they built a hill station during their hundred-year rule of Vietnam. After independence, some of these crops were lost and have only been revived relatively recently.

MEAT

Traditionally, Vietnamese cuisine centred on rice and vegetables, with meat being more of a condiment; today, however, consumption of pork, poultry and beef are all on the rise.

THE MEATIFICATION OF VIETNAM

Vietnam's per-capita consumption of meat is still far less than in the US or UK, but this is changing: today, the average Vietnamese eats four times more meat per year than in the 1980s. The reasons behind this increasingly carnivorous culture are varied: people are eating out more and restaurants or street-food meals tend to offer more meat-heavy options; the average Vietnamese also has access to an increased number of supermarkets which stock frozen, imported meats. Other factors include rising levels of affluence and urbanisation, and the status associated with eating meat.

PORK

A national favourite, pork (*thịt heo*) accounts for nearly 75% of Vietnam's total meat consumption. Neighbouring China may well have influenced this preference: the world's top pork-consuming country, it's a place where eating pork is seen as a symbol of overcoming poverty. Pigs are also handy to have around – they don't take up much space, and will happily consume nearly everything fed to them, from discarded food scraps to parts of crops inedible to humans.

PORK-BASED DISHES

In Vietnam, almost every part of the pig is eaten. The skin is finely shredded and mixed with roasted rice powder to add texture to broken-rice dishes, while the ears add a cartilage crunch to salads and stir-fries. Pigs' feet are slow-cooked in stews and soups, while organ meats are stewed in coconut milk, soy sauce and five-spice powder and eaten with egg noodles or baguettes. The rest of the pig is used for popular dishes such as:

CARAMELISED PORK

(thịt heo kho)

Pork belly's high fat content makes it ideal for this staple dish, cooked down with coconut water, fish sauce and burnt sugar. Boiled eggs, white radish, pineapple and bamboo shoots can also be added.

CHAR SIU PORK

(thịt heo xá xíu)

Reddish slabs of roasted pork shoulder, marinated in five-spice powder, garlic and honey; look for them hanging from hooks in glass cases. Char siu, alongside crispy roasted pork (*thịt heo quay*), are often sold by the kilo; try smaller portions of both in a bánh mì sandwich.

FERMENTED PORK

(nem chua)

Fermented for 3–5 days, with slices of garlic and chilli on top, these little bite-sized packets wrapped in banana leaves contain minced pork, pork skin, roasted rice powder, guava or fig leaves, garlic and spices.

HEADCHEESE

(giò thủ)

A northern favourite, this isn't a cheese at all, but a kind of brawn or terrine made from various parts of a pig's head, including the ears, snout, tongue and cheek, which are cooked with aromatics, fish sauce and wood-ear mushrooms and wrapped up in a banana leaf. Bound together by natural aspic released during the cooking process, the finished product is crunchy with cartilage and is eaten as a snack with pickled onions.

STIR-FRIED PORK WITH PICKLED MUSTARD GREENS

(thịt heo xào cải chua)

The greens add a contrasting touch of sourness and crunch to the fatty pork belly.

© FabVietnam_Photography / Getty Images

Above: Sticky and delicious caramelised pork

© Bloomberg / Getty Images

Above: Pork also features in popular noodle dishes like *bún chả*

POULTRY

The consumption of chicken (and, to a far lesser extent, duck) is growing in Vietnam, with about one million tons of poultry produced annually (as well as some 11 billion eggs), mostly in small-scale households and farms.

CHICKEN AND DUCK DISHES

As with pigs, the Vietnamese use every part of the chicken (*gà*) or duck (*vit*), from head-on birds boiled whole to cartilage and feet. Common dishes include:

BOILED CHICKEN

(gà luộc)

Boiled chicken is eaten with rice and a ginger-laced fish sauce, hand torn into a cabbage and herb salad with lime and fish sauce, or used in a noodle soup with thin, translucent bean-thread noodles.

CRISPY-FRIED CARTILAGE

(sụn gà chiên giòn)

Coated in flour and spices and deep-fried, this addictively crunchy snack is a favourite among kids and beer-drinkers.

CHICKEN FEET

(chân gà)

Skin-on chicken feet are often cooked in a bold, flavourful sauce with ginger, chilli, lemongrass and lime leaves, and pair well with a cold beer. They can also add crunch to salads.

CURRY CHICKEN

(cà ri gà)

Not as spice-heavy as Indian curry and without the heat of Thai curry, the Vietnamese version (most often with chicken) is layered with turmeric, curry leaf, cardamom and other spices, and lots of coconut milk; it's served with rice noodles or a baguette.

A FREE RANGE

The Vietnamese have a strong preference for free-range over commercially raised chickens; they tend to be skinnier and their meat chewier, but are more flavourful thanks to a diverse diet and extra muscle from running around.

DUCK SOUP WITH BAMBOO SHOOTS

(bún măng vịt)

Hearty soup made from a whole duck boiled with ginger, onion and spring onions; bamboo shoots add a pleasantly mild bitterness and chewy texture. It's served with a diluted fish sauce and ginger dipping sauce.

DUCK STEWED IN FERMENTED BEAN CURD

(vịt nấu chao)

Chunks of fermented bean curd lend an umami hit to this hearty stew of duck and taro, eaten over rice noodles.

© galitskaya / Getty Images

Above: Ducks and eggs for sale at a poultry stall

FISH-SAUCE CHICKEN WINGS

(cánh gà chiên nước mắm)

Crispy wings, tossed in a glaze of fish sauce and caramelised sugar for a salty-sweet snack.

FRIED CHICKEN

(gà rán)

KFC is one of the few fast-food chains that has thrived in Vietnam, and there are also an increasing number of streetside stalls with glass cases of fried chicken and fries.

GINGER CHICKEN

(gà kho gừng)

Braised and caramelised in a clay pot, with a generous amount of fresh ginger and coconut water, this rustic dish is a real favourite.

ROASTED CHICKEN

(gà nướng)

Roadside rotisseries churn out whole chickens, ready to be chopped into pieces and eaten with slices of pickled green papaya and a salt, pepper and kumquat dipping sauce.

Chicken or duck?

Duck eggs are almost as widespread as chicken eggs, and you'll often be offered a choice between the two. Duck eggs are often preferred for frying as they're larger and have a creamier, deeper yellow yolk.

BLACK CHICKEN

No, you aren't seeing things! Some Vietnamese dishes use meat from the silkie chicken, a breed with fluffy white plumage but dark bluish-grey or even black meat and bones. Traditionally free-range, silkie (gà ác) *is believed to be healthier than regular chicken, and stars in a nutritious soup* (gà tần thuốc bắc) *made with spices and traditional Chinese medicinal herbs.*

© pirjek / Getty Images

Above: Free-grazing buffalo in northwest Vietnam

BEEF

Although beef consumption is on the rise, the average Vietnamese eats just 3kg (6.6lb) per year. Hot weather, limited grazing and an underdeveloped cattle industry means that much of the beef sold in supermarkets is imported from Australia and the USA.

BUFFALO JERKY

*If you find yourself in northwestern Vietnam, look out for smoked buffalo (*thịt trâu gác bếp*). Marinated in dried chillies and wild forest pepper, the wood-smoked strips of chewy buffalo meat are a speciality of hill-tribe minority groups.*

BEEF DISHES

The average Vietnamese family are unlikely to cook bone-in steaks at home, but several dishes make economical use of beef (*bò*).

BEEF JERKY

(khô bò)

Marinated with lemongrass, garlic, powdered chilli and five-spice powder, Vietnamese jerky is very dry and is eaten as a snack or used as a topping for mango and green papaya salads.

BEEF STEW

(bò kho)

Chunks of brisket and tendon, stewed slowly with carrots and spices including cinnamon, turmeric, cloves and coriander and fennel seeds; it's eaten over egg noodles or with a baguette, used to sop up the rich broth.

GRILLED BEEF IN PIPER LOLOT LEAVES

(bò nướng lá lốt)

One of the dishes that forms Vietnam's classic *bò bảy món* combo ('beef seven ways'), this is minced beef seasoned with lemongrass and shallots, which is wrapped in leaves of the piper lolot herb and chargrilled, before being enfolded again in rice paper alongside fresh herbs, rice noodles, green onion oil and a fermented fish sauce dressing.

ROASTED VEAL

(bê thui)

After being spit-roasted over coals, the meat of a whole calf is thinly sliced and wrapped in rice paper along with fresh herbs and pickles, then dipped in a fermented fish sauce with ginger and sesame seeds.

SHAKEN BEEF

(bò lúc lắc)

Likely influenced by the French, dice-sized cubes of beef (*lúc lắc* can mean 'shake' or 'dice') are quickly sautéed with sliced onions and peppers, and eaten with rice or French fries.

SIZZLING BEEF

(bò né)

Thinly sliced steak, fried egg, a hunk of pâté and French fries are served atop a hot iron plate, sometimes with a simple side salad and a baguette. The word *né* means 'dodge', warning diners to beware of the splashes of hot oil that inevitably come off the sizzling plate

BEEF SEVEN WAYS

Bò bảy món *('beef seven ways') began in a 1930s Mekong Delta restaurant that specialised in traditional beef dishes. Initially, one was served per day, but as customers couldn't wait a full week for their favourites, they began cooking all seven daily. You can order just one dish at today's* bò bảy món *places, but the full seven courses are usually served in this order:*

Bò nhúng giấm Raw slices of lean beef, plunged into a hot-pot with vinegar stock, then rolled in rice paper with unripe banana, star fruit and fresh herbs, and finally dipped in fermented fish sauce with crushed pineapple.

Chả đùm A large meatball of seasoned minced beef, bean-thread noodles and wood-ear mushrooms, wrapped in caul fat (intestine membrane) and steamed, to be scooped up with crispy sesame or shrimp crackers.

Bò cuốn mỡ chài Minced beef seasoned with lemongrass, five-spice powder and other spices, wrapped in caul fat like a small sausage and grilled.

Bò nướng lá lốt Grilled beef in piper lolot leaves.

Bò sa tế Grilled beef, marinated in a spicy *sate* mixture of minced lemongrass, garlic, shallots and chillies; no peanuts, unlike Thai-style *sate*.

Bò bít-tết Similar to sizzling beef (*bò né*) but with a thicker cut of steak.

Cháo bò If you're not stuffed by the sixth course, the final course of rice congee with minced beef aims to put you over the line.

FISH AND

With a long coastline and multitude of ponds and rivers, it's not surprising that fish and seafood loom large in the cuisine of Vietnam – the average Vietnamese consumes nearly as much fish and seafood as pork, chicken and beef combined.

Fishy favourites

BARRAMUNDI

(cá chẽm)

Also known as Asian sea bass, *cá chẽm* is prized for its meaty texture and clean flavour. A great vehicle for absorbing other flavours, it's often simmered in soy sauce or deep-fried and topped with a sweet-and-sour sauce of tomatoes and pineapple.

BASA FISH

(cá basa)

This smooth-skinned catfish is widely farmed in the Mekong Delta. Slightly sweet, its delicate, meaty flesh with few bones is good for caramelising, and also features in sweet-and-sour soups.

GOBY

(cá kèo/cá bống)

Caught in the fresh and brackish waters of the Mekong Delta, spiny goby (*cá kèo*) has tender flesh that's good for hot-pot cooking or braising in a clay pot with Vietnamese mint. The related gobiiformes (*cá bống*) are popular braised with coconut water, caramelised in a clay pot, or crispy fried.

PERCH

(cá rô)

This meaty freshwater fish works well grilled with lemongrass, fried until crispy with a side of mango salad, or sautéed in a sauce of tomato and pickled greens.

MACKEREL

(cá thu)

The mackerel's firm flesh is often pan-fried in a sauce of tomatoes or tamarind.

RED TILAPIA

(cá diêu hồng)

With its sweet, mild taste, tilapia – common in the Mekong Delta – is often used in soups, or steamed with ginger or soy sauce.

SNAKEHEAD

(cá lóc)

An invasive species in some countries, snakehead can be found in freshwater ponds, canals and rice fields throughout Vietnam. Firm with a mild flavour, it's added to sweet-and-sour soup, grilled whole and wrapped in rice paper, or steamed with bottle gourd.

SEAFOOD

BARRAMUNDI

PERCH

BASA FISH

GOBY

seafood

Opposite: Fresh-caught fish on sale in Hue

Seafood is often steamed with beer, coconut water or lemongrass to preserve the natural sweetness, and accompanied by a salt, pepper and lime juice dipping sauce; wok-frying tends to include bolder flavours like tangy tamarind or Singapore-style tomato and egg.

If the seafood section of restaurant menus only lists the proteins, the quoted price includes cooking to order using your preferred method of preparation. Some common seafood options include:

ABALONE

(bào ngư)

Similar in taste to scallops, but with a chewier, meatier quality, sizeable abalone are sliced thinly and eaten raw, sashimi-style, or grilled with green onion oil.

CLAMS

Regular clams (*ngao*) and razor clams (*ốc móng tay*) are grilled and topped with green onion oil and peanuts, wok-fried with fresh herbs in oyster sauce, or steamed with lemongrass; the strikingly red flesh of blood clams (sò huyết) is due to high haemoglobin levels. If the shells are small, a metal pick will usually be provided.

CRAB

(cua)

Vietnam has fresh- and saltwater crabs. The former are smaller and are often pickled or crispy-fried as a snack.
The larger saltwater varieties generally have large pincers and a mono-coloured, round shell which turns dark orange when cooked; *ghẹ* usually have white spots on the shell and include blue and red swimming crabs and stone crabs. You might also see soft-shelled crabs, usually deep-fried then wrapped with herbs in a lettuce leaf and dipped in *nước chấm*. Crab is also wok-fried with tamarind or simply steamed in the shell.

LOBSTER

(tôm hùng)

Grilled lobster topped with cheese has become popular in recent years; it's also wok-fried with tamarind or deep-fried then tossed in salt, pepper, sugar and garlic

OYSTERS

(hàu)

Vietnam's coastal waters produce 15,000 tons of oysters per year; they're often grilled (topped with green onion oil or cheese) or added to salads.

SQUID

(mực)

Sun-dried squid is very chewy (you'll feel it in your jaw the day after) and is best washed down with a cold beer. Fresh squid is popular grilled, fried with butter and garlic, or deep-fried.

TIGER PRAWNS

(tôm sú)

Giant tiger prawns are often cooked head-on and shell-on, steamed in lemongrass, grilled or deep-fried, sometimes with salted egg yolk.

© HNH Images / Getty Images

VIETNAMESE FISH CAKES

Fish cakes (chả cá) are a popular way to eat mackerel, basa or perch. The fish is finely minced or scraped off the bone with a spoon and mixed with dill, shallots, sugar and fish sauce; the resultant cakes are steamed or fried and eaten as a snack, or added to soups.

DRIED FISH

All along Vietnam's coastline and throughout its deltas you'll see bamboo racks covered in fish laid out to dry. Simply marinated in salt, pepper and chilli, the fish are rehydrated for use in soup stocks, as well as being grilled or added to salads and fried rice.

© Greg Elms / Lonely Planet

Above: Tabletop cooking at Hanoi's renowned Chả Cá Lã Vọng restaurant

© bbq / Shutterstock

Above: Hanoian *chả cá*, ready to eat

The street that fish built

Tucked into Hanoi's Old Quarter, Chả Cá Street is something of a culinary oddity. Traditionally, the lanes of this photogenic area are named after the craft guilds that once serviced the royal palace; Chả Cá Street is unique in being named after a dish.

The fishy association started more than a century ago, when a restaurant owned and run by the Doan family began serving *chả cá*, chunks of fish marinated in turmeric and galangal and cooked with dill. The fabulous *chả cá* that they cooked up became so famous that the entire street was eventually renamed from Hàng Sơn ('Lacquer Street', where riverboats were waterproofed) to Chả Cá.

A BOWL OF CHẢ CÁ

Today, the Doan's original one-dish restaurant still stands at 14 Chả Cá Street; it's named after 11th-century Chinese noble Lã Vọng, whose statue (fishing rod in hand) stands outside the door. Climb the wooden stairs to the dining room, where the windows are perpetually thrown open to the narrow street below, and prepare to enjoy some *chả cá*. Before cooking, the chunks of fish (traditionally catfish from the Lo or Da rivers, but snakehead can also be used) are marinated in fermented rice and shrimp paste, plus turmeric, galangal and other aromatics, and then lightly grilled over charcoal. The fish is then finished with green onions and fresh dill in a pan atop a portable stove right at the table, adding a fun DIY element. Add the piping-hot fish to a bowl of rice noodles, fresh herbs and roasted peanuts, drizzle over a pungent sauce of fermented shrimp paste and lime juice, and eat with crispy grilled rice-paper crackers. For a true *chả cá* experience, ask for a few drops of *cà cuống* extract (a fragrant water-bug pheromone – much better than it sounds!) to be added to the sauce.

While the roots of many dishes popular in Hanoi can be traced back to neighbouring provinces, *chả cá* is the city's iconic meal – fussy to make and fussy to eat, but proudly 100% Hanoian.

UNUSUAL FOODS

While 'unusual' is firmly in the eye of the beholder, there are some Vietnamese delicacies that the average visitor may find anything but ordinary.

BALUT

Fertilised, unhatched duck eggs (*hột vịt lộn*), boiled and spooned out from in the shell and accompanied by Vietnamese mint, a salt-and-pepper dipping sauce and a squeeze of lime.

BLOOD PRODUCTS

Made from uncooked duck or pig blood mixed with a salt-water or fish-sauce solution to prevent coagulation, blood pudding (*tiết canh*) also includes boiled ear, cartilage, heart and liver, along with peanuts and fresh herbs. If you find something that looks like tofu in your soup or congee, but is dark purplish-maroon, it's likely a cube of cooked blood (*huyết* or *tiết*)

COCONUT WORM

The larvae of the Asian palm weevil, coconut worms (*đuông dừa*) grow fat from the young shoots of the coconut tree. A speciality of the Mekong Delta, they are deep-fried, boiled in coconut water or eaten with sticky rice.

DOG AND CAT MEAT

Despite calls for a ban, some five million dogs are eaten annually in Vietnam, mostly in the north. Gamey dog meat (*thịt chó* or *thịt cầy*) is paired with strong flavours like lemongrass, galangal, fermented rice and fermented shrimp paste. Cat meat is less common; it's mostly limited to the city of Thai Binh, and restaurants will often use the euphemism 'tiny tiger' (*tiểu hổ*). Dog and cat meat are often an accompaniment to beer or other alcohol.

JELLYFISH

Translucent and crunchy, jellyfish (*sứa*) are sometimes included in cucumber, mango and carrot salads.

MEDICINAL WINE

Rượu thuốc is rice wine with fruits, leaves and roots added for medicinal purposes; some versions feature snakes, lizards and seahorses (usually whole), as well as animal parts like penis, testicle and bile sac.

RAT

Definitely not the city sewer-dwelling kind, edible rats (*chuột đồng*) fatten up in Vietnam's rice fields. Crispy-fried with fish sauce or lemongrass, or dusted in five-spice powder and grilled, field rats are said to have sweet, rabbit-like flesh, and to be good for the bones.

PHỞ

If Vietnam were to have a national dish as beloved outside the country as within, it would be phở. Traditionally a breakfast staple, phở is now available at any time of day, from streetside carts to upscale restaurants. Regarded as a hangover cure and a comfort food, this beef-based noodle soup is certainly a cheap, fast and filling one-bowl meal.

PHỞ THROUGH THE AGES

Despite its popularity at home and abroad, there is some uncertainty as to how phở came about. The general consensus puts its origins around Hanoi or Nam Dinh in northern Vietnam, somewhere between 1900 and 1910, when the first photos and references to this soul-satisfying soup appeared.

The more fanciful origin stories revolve around a Vietnamese woman who wanted to please her French lover by making the classic Gallic pot-au-feu, a hearty stew of beef shanks and rump roast simmered for hours with marrowbones and vegetables. Unfamiliar with the flavours, she added locally available cinnamon, star anise and cloves instead of parsley, thyme and bay leaves – and voilà! To add more fuel to the culinary conspiracy theory, the French word for fire – 'feu' – is pronounced almost exactly the same as the Vietnamese 'phở', inferring that this hallowed soup's name might be a loaned word. Another story says that phở originated with Chinese cooks who sold soup on the streets of Hanoi, using flat rice noodles (*phan* in Chinese) rather than the thinner Vietnamese vermicelli noodles.

The truth probably lies somewhere in between. It's said that in the early 20th century, a hearty buffalo meat and vermicelli-noodle soup, *xáo trâu*, was popular among sailors and dockworkers along the Red River. Because beef bones suddenly became cheap and plentiful (an unwanted by-product of carving up beef to serve to French colonists), beef replaced buffalo in the soup; the Chinese added their broad noodles, and phở was born.

Above: Beef phở, Vietnam's de facto national dish

REGIONAL VARIATIONS

Traditionally, a good bowl of phở comprises a clear broth made with genuine beef bones, stewed for at least six hours and with no other meats mixed in. It must also have long, unbroken strips of flat rice noodles, plus thinly sliced, well-done brisket, and the barest of seasonings to showcase the meaty, beefy broth. Today, however, the question of what makes a perfect phở varies from region to region, and from household to household. And while many cities have famous phở restaurants, they're usually known for their longevity or specific history rather than the superior taste of their soup – Ho Chi Minh City's Phở Bình is a prime example, having gained its notoriety by serving as a base for northern Vietnamese operatives to smuggle weaponry during the American War.

ANYONE PHỞ COCKTAILS?

Innovative bars across Vietnam are taking inspiration from everyone's favourite noodle soup. Ho Chi Minh City's rooftop NHAU NHAU bar serves a 'phojito', combining phở flavours with rice spirits and topped with a charred stick of cinnamon and fresh herbs; their bullshot includes a dash of phở broth alongside Worcestershire sauce, sriracha, lime and rice wine.

THE EVOLUTION OF PHỞ

Over the decades, phở has changed and adapted to the times. A meatless variety, cheekily called phở không người lái *('without a driver') emerged during the difficult years around WWII, while phở made with chicken bones became popular when beef was scarce. Thanks to the Geneva Accords, a million northern Vietnamese moved south in 1954, bringing phở with them – where it got a Saigonese makeover.*

Finding the perfect phở

Ordering a bowl of phở is a straightforward affair, but it pays to get a handle on the following basic principles.

THE BROTH

Phở starts out with the bones, which are simmered for anywhere between three and 12 hours to draw out all the flavour; aromatics like cinnamon sticks, star anise, cloves, coriander seeds, the ginger-like *thảo quả* and roasted ginger and onion go into the pot, too. Chicken and beef phở don't just differ in the protein – the broth is also cooked with the respective bones, meaning it's uncommon for a place to serve both varieties. Because of its long cooking time and sheer amount of ingredients needed, phở is usually eaten out rather than made at home – most Vietnamese get their phở fix from one of the many small outlets in their local neighbourhood.

© Francoise De Mulder / Getty Images

HANOI OR SOUTHERN-STYLE?

Phở was originally a northern Vietnamese creation, but this Hanoi-style phở (also called *phở bắc*) is often considered bland by southern standards – it's focused on the clarity and flavour of the broth, which is made without any fat and few sauces or seasonings so as not to obscure the natural goodness of the bones and marrow. Popular accompaniments in the north include a stick of fried dough known as *bánh quẩy*, plus finely chopped lime leaves for chicken phở. Ho Chi Minh City-style phở is sweeter, served with lots of fresh herbs and bean sprouts; phở noodles tend to be thinner in the south, too. Wherever you are, a sign will usually tell you what style of phở is being served.

THE BASICS OF THE BOWL

Ordering phở starts with choosing your proteins. Even with chicken phở, picky eaters can choose breast, thigh, skin and other parts of the bird; if you don't specify, the seller will simply handpick pieces for you. For beef, non-adventurous eaters can go with the plainest option, slices of well-done brisket (*phở chín*); another popular choice is thin, raw slices of steak (*tái*), which you can press down into your soup to flash-cook in the hot broth.

Other options include beef meatballs (*bò viên*), flank (*nạm*), fatty brisket (*gầu*), tendon (*gân*) and tripe (*sách*). Eateries will also have a 'special' version (*đặc biệt*), with a little bit of everything. If you can't find what you want on the

© Matt Munro / Lonely Planet

Opposite: A bowl of phở on the go
Right: Phở bò dressed with herbs

menu (or if there isn't one, as is often the case), simply point to what you want from the spread of prepared meats, which are usually in a glass case. Less common additions include a raw egg cracked into your soup, an extra bowl of liquid fat that's been skimmed off the top (*nước béo*), or some concentrated broth (*nước tiết*); the protein-rich latter option is especially popular with pregnant women.

With proteins chosen, the seller will start assembling the bowl, blanching the noodles so they don't cool down the broth, adding meat and green onions, sliced onions and coriander.

FINESSING THE FLAVOUR

Personalising your bowl of phở comes down to individual taste – start by taking a sip of the broth. Too bland? Add a few drops of undiluted fish sauce, a dash of pepper, or some sweetish hoisin sauce. Too sweet? Add a squeeze of lime or some of the pickled garlic often found in Hanoi-style phở joints. Want more heat? There's usually a bottle of chilli sauce, a container of intense *sate* or sliced bird's eye chilli. Phở places will also have little dishes for creating your own sauce for dipping the meat or meatballs, usually a combination of hoisin and chilli.

CHOOSE YOUR ADD-ONS

Now it's time to tackle the herbs and sprouts. Raw bean sprouts add some nice crunch, but you can also ask that they be blanched first. If it's your first time encountering the accompanying fresh herbs, give them a little taste before stripping off the leaves and adding them to your bowl. While they'll taste stronger raw, pushing them down into the hot soup releases the oils and mellows out the flavours. Out of the usual trio of basil, sawtooth coriander and rice-paddy herb, the latter has the most pungent flavour so you might want to use it judiciously at first.

SUPER-SIZED PHỞ

Returning Vietnamese have opened up their own restaurants serving American-style phở, which tends to be slightly sweeter and usually in bigger portions. For giant USA-sized bowls, look for places serving phở xe lửa *or* phở tàu bay *(literally 'train phở' and 'airplane phở'). You'll pay double the price of any local phở, but the setting is usually appealing and you'll certainly leave full.*

VARIATIONS ON PHỞ

Right: Vietnamese woman selling famous *phở bo* noodle soup

If you simply can't get enough of phở, you can try these variations, many of them more popular in Hanoi than Ho Chi Minh City.

Instant phở This supermarket noodle-aisle staple is a poor imitation, but quick and convenient in a pinch (or to bring home as a souvenir); it's best if you add your own meat and fresh herbs.

Mixed phở (phở trộn) Phở noodles combined with crispy-fried shallots, peanuts and coriander, typically topped with chicken rather than beef, and served alongside a little bowl of chicken broth with a bit of soy sauce, lime juice, sugar and minced garlic.

Phở burger A favourite at restaurants catering to expats, phở burgers use crispy-fried rice noodles in place of a bun; a beef patty infused with phở flavours; basil, bean sprouts and other herbs instead of lettuce; and a hoisin- and chilli-based sauce.

Phở rolls (phở cuốn) Steamed rice paper wrapped around beef, sprouts and herbs, and dipped in a fish sauce dressing.

Phở stew (phở sốt vang) Halfway between a phở noodle soup and the heartier beef stew known as *bò kho*, this is chunks of beef cooked with tomatoes, onions and typical phở spices, and served over phở noodles.

Stir-fried phở (phở xào) Phở noodles, pan-fried with beef, carrots, tomatoes and leaf mustard in a brown sauce. A close cousin is *phở áp chảo*, in which the noodles are pan-fried separately until crispy before serving with the stir-fried beef and vegetables; in *phở chiên phồng*, the noodles are deep-fried into delicious golden pillows of dough.

THE PHONETICS OF PHỞ

Not 'fur'. Not 'foe'. The correct way to pronounce the name of Vietnam's iconic noodle soup is something like 'fuh' – though you need to add the right tone, too: the 'fuh' should sound like a question that dips and then rises.

VIETNAMESE SOUPS

There is a world of Vietnamese soup aside from phở. Home-cooked meals are typically accompanied by *canh*, a simple blend of melon, squash or leafy greens in a broth flavoured with bones or dried salted fish or shrimp, and there are plenty of soups that are fantastic in their own right.

Above: *Bún mắm* is an intense Mekong Delta speciality

© Leisa Tyler / Alamy Stock Photo

BÁNH CANH

Fat, udon-like noodles made from rice and tapioca flours, in a soup with soft and chewy proteins such as picked crab meat or an entire crab, pork knuckle, fish cakes, shrimp, quail's eggs or sliced boiled pork.

BÚN BÒ HUẾ

A spicy noodle soup originating in the former imperial city, with a rich broth of beef bones and shank flavoured with lemongrass, chilli oil and shrimp paste, plus pig's knuckles, cubes of congealed pig's blood, tendons, beef brisket and slices of steamed pork sausage. *Bún bò* is the non-spicy version.

BÚN MẮM

This Mekong Delta speciality, with a strong smell and a bold taste, is thought to have originated in Cambodia; it's a memorable mixture of fermented fish with rice noodles, shrimp, fish, squid or roasted pork.

BÚN MỌC

With its roots in the cool highlands of northern Vietnam, this comforting noodle soup consists of a pork-bone broth topped with meatballs made from minced pork and wood-ear mushrooms, or perhaps short ribs, steamed pork ham and bamboo shoots.

BÚN RIÊU

This unique noodle soup has a richly layered broth thanks to pork bones, tomatoes, freshwater crab roe and fermented fish paste. Other ingredients are added according to region: snails in the north and steamed pork sausage in central Vietnam; the Ho Chi Minh City version includes tamarind, chunks of fried tofu and pig's blood, and cakes made from crab meat, dried shrimp and minced pork.

BÚN THANG

This pretty northern favourite consists of a clear chicken- and pork-bone broth with vermicelli rice noodles topped by a rainbow of colours: julienned egg crepes, steamed pork ham, shredded chicken and green onions.

CAO LẦU

Unique to Hoi An due to its distinctively thick, chewy noodles (made by soaking the rice in alum-rich lye water), this soupy noodle dish is unlike any other, topped with five-spice-flavoured pork, crunchy crackers and a heap of fresh herbs, and served in a bit of broth.

© Megan Ahrens / Getty Images

Above: *Cao lâu*, a tasty soup/noodle-bowl hybrid from Hoi An

MAKE A DOUBLE MEAL OF IT

***Hủ tiếu** can either be ordered with broth (nước) or dry (khô). If ordered dry, the noodles are tossed with soy and oyster sauces and the broth is served on the side. It's like getting two meals in one!*

HỦ TIẾU

A noodle soup with Chinese origins, featuring thin, chewy rice noodles in a pork-based broth simmered with carrots and turnips for extra sweetness. Toppings include minced or sliced pork and pork offal, with a side of fresh bean sprouts and herbs. Nam Vang (Phnom Penh) is known for a Cambodian-style *hủ tiếu*; Mỹ Tho's has seafood and extra-chewy noodles; and Sa Đéc *hủ tiếu* has the area's characteristic long, squarish noodles.

MÌ QUẢNG

This Quang Nam province noodle dish (albeit with less broth than most soups) started out as a labourer's meal that turned leftovers into a hearty breakfast. Turmeric-yellow rice noodles are topped with shrimp, pork, chicken, fish or beef, and served with a rice and toasted sesame seed cracker.

MÌ

While it technically means 'wheat noodles', *mì* is a catchall that can include soups with yellow wheat or egg noodles. Often sold from wheeled carts, *mì* typically comprises a pork bone and root vegetable broth with char siu pork, wontons and pork knuckle.

MIẾN GÀ

The ultimate comfort food, this simple chicken soup has a fragrant broth made by boiling chicken bones with star anise, ginger, charred onions and fish sauce. The deboned meat is served atop glass noodles, with coriander and green onions.

Right: Building a bánh mì

BÁNH MÌ

While bánh mì can refer to any kind of bread, it's usually understood to be the French-style baguettes, sold out of big woven baskets and glass cases throughout Vietnam and used to make the classic Vietnamese sandwich.

THE BACKGROUND TO BÁNH MÌ

A legacy of French colonisation, the baguette has been adapted to the tastes of the Vietnamese since it was introduced here in the middle of the 19th century. Perhaps as a result of being included in Saigon school lunches around the 1950s, bánh mì became smaller, airier and with a thinner, crispier crust than their French predecessors. Nowadays, commercially made bánh mì typically only have five ingredients: bread flour (and not a mix of wheat and rice flour as some claim), water, yeast, salt and bread improver – no sugar, butter or eggs.

Some say that the Vietnamese bánh mì sandwich was inspired by the French pan bagnat, a quick, portable sandwich of simple ingredients like tuna and anchovies, vegetables and sliced boiled eggs. Today's bánh mì bread serves as a wonderfully light vehicle for all manner of fillings, and often appears in lists of the world's best sandwiches.

BÒ NÉ

Popular in the mornings, bò né *(and the similar northern dish,* bánh mì chảo*) is a hodgepodge of French-inspired ingredients like marinated steak slices, pâté, a fried egg and French fries, all served atop a sizzling-hot steel plate, and mopped up with a baguette.*

© hxyume / Getty Images

SYMPHONY IN A SANDWICH

Whether eaten for breakfast, lunch or dinner, default bánh mì ingredients include butter (although the dairy-less Vietnamese version that doesn't melt in the heat is more like a mayo of egg yolks, oil and lime juice), plus pork-liver pâté, cucumber batons, sprigs of coriander, pickled carrot and daikon, and a final topping of fresh chilli or chilli sauce, plus a splash of soy or fish sauce or meat/tomato gravy. Common proteins include:

Cold meats (*thịt nguội*) Steamed pork belly – half meat, half fat, with a reddish skin.
Crispy roast pork (*heo quay*) Five-spice-marinated pork belly with a crispy crackling.
Fish cakes (*chả cá*) Seasoned minced fish, deep-fried into strips or patties.
Fried eggs (*trứng ốp-la*) Fried eggs cooked to order, common at breakfast time.
Grilled pork (*thịt nướng*) Skewers of grilled pork.
Meat floss (*ruốc* in the north, *chà bông* in the south) Usually cooked chicken or pork, fork-shredded then pan-fried over low heat until dry and fluffy.
Minced pork sausage (*chả lụa*) A chewy, mild-tasting sausage, wrapped in banana leaves and steamed.
Pork meatballs (*xíu mại*) Steamed meatballs in a brown gravy.
Sardines (*cá mòi*) Sardines in oil, unadorned from the can they came in.
Shredded roasted chicken (*gà xé*) Chicken breast roasted with a simple seasoning.
Shredded pork skin (*bì*) Seasoned with roasted rice powder, which adds a pleasant crunch.
Tofu Crispy-fried, a common vegetarian option.

BÒ KHO AND BAGUETTE

As well as their role in bánh mì, baguettes are the usual accompaniment to bò kho, a rich beef and carrot stew flavoured with lemongrass, star anise, turmeric, coriander seed and cinnamon.

Above: *Bánh khọt*
Opposite, from top: *Bánh khọt; bánh cân*

BÁNH

While the word *bánh* in Vietnamese is often translated as cake, it's actually a classifier that points to anything (savoury or sweet) made from flour (any type of flour), in any shape and using any cooking method.

© epixx / Getty Images

SAVOURY BÁNH

'Bánh' is usually qualified by another word: add 'wheat' it's a baguette (bánh mì); add 'phở' and it's the broad rice noodles that go with the soup (*bánh phở*); add the word for 'sizzling' and it's a turmeric-tinged savoury crepe stuffed with pork and shrimp (*bánh xèo*). Incredibly diverse, the savoury *bánh* below make for a great snack or meal.

DEEP-FRIED DUMPLINGS

(bánh gối)

Popular in northern Vietnam, these samosa-like crispy dumplings (the name means 'pillow cakes', after their half-moon shape) are encased in a wheat-flour batter and filled with minced pork, wood-ear mushrooms, bean-thread noodles, Chinese sausage and a chicken or quail egg.

FRIED RICE CAKES

(bánh khọt)

A sort of mini-pancake, made from a rice- or tapioca-flour batter (sometimes with egg), which is poured into individual oiled wells in a metal mould, topped with a whole shrimp and 'fried' atop a brazier. To eat them, wrap in the accompanying fresh greens and herbs, and dip into *nước chấm* sauce.

GRILLED RICE CAKES

(bánh căn)

Popular in south-central Vietnam and, like *bánh khọt*, made with a rice-flour batter poured into individual wells in an earthenware mould which is set over a brazier. The little cakes are topped with shrimp, minced pork and green onion oil, and typically accompanied by shredded green mango, cucumber and star fruit, plus *nước chấm* dipping sauce. Boiled eggs, fish cakes and minced pork meatballs can also accompany.

RICE NOODLES WITH COCONUT MILK

(bánh tằm bì)

Named after the silkworms (*tằm*) that they resemble, these thick, round rice and tapioca noodles are topped with shredded pork skin and fresh herbs. A dollop of coconut milk and roasted peanuts go on top, and a bowl of *nước chấm* sauce accompanies this strangely delicious, sweet-and-savoury dish.

© Nguyen Cuong / Getty Images

Below, from left: *Bánh khọt; bánh ít; bánh cuốn; bánh bao*

© Muk Photo / Shutterstock

© Nguy?n Thanh Phong / Alamy Stock Photo

SHRIMP CRACKERS

(bánh phồng tôm)

This crunchy snack or salad accompaniment is a familiar staple of Vietnamese restaurants the world over. The crackers are made by grinding fresh shrimp, tapioca flour and spices into a thin sheet, which is dried and then deep-fried.

STEAMED BUNS

(bánh bao)

Introduced to Vietnam by Cantonese immigrants, these steamed buns are made with a dough of wheat-flour, yeast, milk and oil, which is wrapped around fillings such as minced pork or Chinese sausage, plus wood-ear mushrooms, bean-thread noodles or an egg. *Bánh bao* are always served hot, and are popular as an on-the-go breakfast – look for them in big steamers or glass cases.

In southern Vietnam, the similar *bánh bao chiên* is a smaller version which is deep-fried rather than steamed.

STEAMED RICE CAKES

(bánh bèo)

A watery rice- and tapioca-flour batter poured into small ceramic dishes and cooked in a steamer. They're served straight from the dishes, each topped with dried shrimp, crispy pork rind and green onion oil, with a *nước chấm* dipping sauce.

STEAMED RICE DUMPLINGS

(bánh giò)

A rice- and tapioca-flour dough with minced pork, shrimp and wood-ear mushrooms, wrapped with a banana leaf into a pyramid-like dumpling and steamed. Soft and delicate, they're eaten with pickled vegetables and soy or chilli sauce.

STEAMED RICE-FLOUR CAKES

(bánh nậm)

A dough of rice-flour and tapioca starch is placed on the smooth side of a banana leaf and topped with minced pork and shrimp; the leaf is then folded into a flat rectangle and steamed.

© Quang Ngo / Alamy Stock Photo

© imageBROKER / Alamy Stock Photo

STEAMED RICE ROLLS

(bánh cuốn)

A pillowy-soft breakfast favourite that is well worth the wait at street stalls. It's made in the same way as rice paper, with a loose batter of rice flour and tapioca starch poured onto a piece of fabric that's stretched over a steamer; once cooked, an oiled stick is used to carefully lift off the sheet and roll it around a filling of sautéed minced pork, wood-ear mushrooms and onion. Cut into bite-sized pieces, *bánh cuốn* is typically served with steamed, fried or fermented pork sausage, blanched bean sprouts, fresh herbs and crispy-fried shallots. Pour the *nước chấm* sauce on top before eating.

For the similar *bánh ướt*, steamed rice-flour sheets are pre-made and served with pork sausage, and sometimes a cupcake-like piece of fried dough and mung beans. There's also a more recent variation of *bánh cuốn* in which egg is added to the batter, creating a fluffier, almost crêpe-like skin.

STEAMED TAPIOCA DUMPLINGS

(bánh bột lọc)

Minced pork belly and shrimp, simmered in sugar and aromatics then wrapped in a tapioca-starch dough and boiled. The translucent cooked dough reveals the tantalisingly orange-coloured filling.

STICKY RICE BALLS

(bánh khúc/xôi khúc)

These rice balls with a pork and mung bean filling get their signature greenish colour from the leaves of wild-growing cudweed. Rolled in grains of sticky rice and steamed, they're always eaten hot.

STICKY RICE DUMPLINGS

(bánh ít)

Wrapped in a banana leaf as per *bánh giò*, *bánh ít* is a glutinous rice dough surrounding sweet or savoury fillings: shredded coconut and sweetened mashed mung beans; or minced pork and shrimp. *Bánh ít trần* ('naked' *bánh ít*) are similar, but rolled into balls and steamed without the banana leaf.

DESSERTS

While Vietnamese savoury food is world class, some may find the sweet course decidedly less so. The Vietnamese palate is a finicky one: Western-style cakes and cookies are often deemed too sweet, but super-sugary condensed milk and sweetened coconut milk figure in many local desserts.

THE SWEET COURSE

In a country where butter and dairy aren't commonly used and home ovens are extremely rare, desserts tend to be steamed, grilled or cooked using ingredients not typically associated with sweet things like beans, corn and taro. The Vietnamese name for dessert is *tráng miệng*, which more describes refreshing the palate than eating something decadent to end a meal; in fact, one of the most popular sweet treats here is a street-food snack, *chè*.

Many restaurants won't even have a dessert section on the menu, but there are some popular puddings that you might encounter.

© robertcicchetti / Getty Images

Above: *Bánh trung thu* **Opposite, from left:** *Bánh bò; bánh tiêu; bánh flan*

BÁNH BÒ

Light, spongy and chewy, this steamed rice- and tapioca-flour cake is made with sugar, coconut milk, yeast and, sometimes, shredded coconut.

BÁNH ĐẬU XANH

These little squares of mashed mung beans, sugar, coconut milk and oil are the perfect accompaniment to hot tea.

BÁNH FLAN

A take on the classic French custard, the Vietnamese version is made with eggs, milk, vanilla, condensed milk and caramelised sugar, all steamed in little cups; a dash of black coffee is sometimes added before serving.

BÁNH KẸP

Often sold streetside, and made in a foldable metal mould over a charcoal brazier, these thin, sweet waffles are sometimes flavoured with pandan leaves.

BÁNH KHOAI MÌ

Finely grated cassava gives this grilled or steamed cake some substance; it's sweetened with condensed milk or coconut milk.

BÁNH TIÊU

A fried, airy pillow of dough made of wheat flour, sugar and vanilla, coated with white sesame seeds. The smaller, denser *bánh cam* or *bánh rán* is made with glutinous rice flour and filled with sweetened mashed mung beans.

BÁNH TRUNG THU

Popular as a gift item during the Mid-Autumn Festival, these 'mooncakes' with a flaky crust can be sweet (filled with lotus seeds, red beans, mung beans and candied melon) or savoury (with salted egg yolks, Chinese sausage and pork floss).

RAU CÂU

An agar-set jelly that comes in many flavours, including coconut, fruit and coffee.

TÀO PHỚ (TÀU HŨ)

Thin layers of silken tofu, served hot in a sugar syrup with slices of ginger and a dollop of coconut milk, and often sold from a yoke.

VIETNAMESE-STYLE PATISSERIE

The Vietnamese have put their own spin on French-inspired baked goods like eclairs, pâté chaud *(flaky puff pastries stuffed with chicken or pork) and* chou à la crème *(custard-filled cream puffs), as well as croissants, which are known as crab bread or buffalo-horn bread for their appearance (and because croissant is hard to pronounce). Look for these inexpensive treats wherever baguettes are sold.*

© iveta kulhava / Shutterstock; Moon Le / Shutterstock; Kyoko Uchida / Alamy Stock Photo

CHÈ

Sometimes described as sweet soup, *chè* is a classic case of the sum being greater than the parts. The most popular of all Vietnamese sweets, these custard-like concoctions can be made from beans, seeds, jelly, fruits or vegetables, put together in an endless variety of combinations and colours, and are usually eaten from a glass with a spoon.

Below: Colourful combinations on offer at a *chè* stall

© James Pham / Lonely Planet

CHÈ VARIETIES

On their own, some *chè* ingredients – chia or basil seeds, seaweed – may seem unusual dessert choices, but in combination, and often with the addition of creamy coconut milk, they can be transformed into a delicious and refreshing dessert.

While there are entire restaurants dedicated just to *chè*, you'll also find it sold from glass cases by the side of the road or from mobile carts. Look for dozens of lidded pots filled with different kinds of *chè*, or hanging pre-filled bags ready to be packed with shaved ice and taken home to enjoy. Some of the most popular types of *chè* include:

Chè bà ba (chè thưng) Chunks of cassava, sweet potato and taro, simmered in coconut milk with tapioca pearls and mung beans, and topped with roasted peanuts.

Chè ba màu This visually appealing tri-coloured *chè* is layered with red kidney beans and yellow mung beans, and topped with strands of green pandan-flavoured jelly and a dollop of sweetened coconut milk. Use the long spoon to mix all the ingredients together before eating.

Chè bắp Kernelled corn is the star of this gloopy *chè*, thickened with arrowroot starch and topped with sweetened coconut milk.

Chè bưởi This unique sweet *chè* combines the bitter, spongy pith of the grapefruit-like pomelo with mung beans, coconut milk and tapioca starch.

Chè chuối A sweet, flavourful Southeast Asian variety of banana (*chuối sứ*), simmered in pandan-flavoured coconut milk with chewy tapioca pearls, and topped with roasted peanuts and sesame seeds – a winning combination. A similar mix with flattened bananas is often put into little bags and frozen for a refreshing popsicle-like treat.

Chè đậu All sorts of earthy beans (mung, adzuki, black-eyed peas, cowpeas), used individually or together, and combined with sugar, coconut milk and starch to thicken.

Chè khúc bạch Refreshing on a hot day, this chilled dessert features cubes of gelatine flavoured with almond extract, and fresh lychees in a sugar syrup.

Chè mè đen Enjoyed cold or hot, and also known as *xí mà phù*, this creamy concoction of black sesame paste thickened with arrowroot is cooked with coconut water, the juice from the pennywort herb and slices of ginger.

Chè sâm bổ lượng Halfway between a soup and a drink, this hodgepodge of ingredients and textures includes slivers of seaweed, fruits (red jujube and dried longan), plus Chinese pearl barley, lotus seeds and sliced lotus root, all in a sugar syrup. Served cold, it's supremely refreshing on a hot day.

Chè sương sa hạt lựu Diced water chestnuts, coated in tapioca starch and soaked in carrot and beetroot juices with pandan leaves make for a colourful presentation, together with sweetened mung beans and coconut milk. Despite the name, it doesn't contain persimmon seeds (*hạt lựu*).

Chè Thái Originating in Thailand, this *chè* is rather unique in its use of seasonal fruit and jellies in sweetened milk. Common toppings include fresh jackfruit, durian, young palm seeds and crunchy water chestnuts.

Chè trôi nước A favourite during Lunar New Year, these glutinous rice dumplings are filled with a sweetened mung-bean paste and served in a sweet, ginger-flavoured syrup, topped with toasted sesame seeds and coconut milk.

Right: Streetside smoothie station

DRINKS

Just as eating is a social – and public – event in Vietnam, so is drinking, whether it's a boozing session with friends while perched on stools outside a bar, or a coffee while striking a business deal in an upmarket café.

SO MANY CHOICES, SO LITTLE TIME

There are some drinks that are iconically Vietnamese: a fresh green coconut with a straw sticking out of it; a beer with a giant piece of ice floating in the glass; a slow-drip *phin* (filter) coffee; or an icy glass of *soda chanh* (lime soda) beaded with condensation. But there's also a dizzying array of other don't-miss Vietnamese drinks, from hand-picked gourmet teas to smoothies, shots of rice wine and locally made craft beers.

Coffee is a big-hitter in the Vietnamese drinks scene. It's an any-time-of-the-day drink here: people will meet for coffee from sunrise until well after sundown, and treat their brew as something to be savoured. It's perfectly normal to take an hour over one glass of *cà phê sữa đá* (coffee with milk and ice) or a *cà phê đen đá* (iced black coffee) while watching the world go by.

The array of blended fruit smoothies and other sweet soft drinks are usually a mid-morning or mid-afternoon treat, or perhaps a night-time alternative for teetotallers; other alcohol-free favourites include iced herbal tea and kumquat-laced sugar-cane juice.

And then there's *đi nhậu* (literally 'going drinking'), a ritual which always involves food alongside the booze: small plates of salty, spicy nibbles are shared by the table and every sip is accompanied by lively toasts. In the countryside, especially in ethnic minority villages and among older folk, rice wine (*rượu*) is the tipple of choice, whether moonshine-style homebrew or a bottle from one of Vietnam's small distilleries. In urban areas, a *nhậu* session starts with locally brewed lager and then moves on to something stronger; and in the big cities you'll also find bars dedicated to wine, cocktails and artisan craft beers.

TAP WATER

Remember: don't drink the tap water. Nước suối *(bottled water) is readily available at supermarkets, markets and corner stores; specify 'lạnh' (cold) if you don't want one of the warm bottles on display in front of a shop. Empty plastic bottles are collected by trash-pickers, who sell them to recycling centres, so always try to separate them out from the rest of your rubbish.*

TEA

Believed to centre the mind, refresh the body and aid digestion, tea – *chè* in the north, *trà* in the south – has been enjoyed in Vietnam for centuries, possibly even before Chinese occupation began in the 2nd century BCE.

Above: Served hot or iced, Vietnamese tea comes in myriad varieties

THE CULTURE OF TEA

In the distant past, Vietnamese farmers drank *chè tươi* (fresh tea) made with leaves plucked from their gardens, boiled with water and served in a common bowl. Drinking tea was considered a social activity, giving friends and family time to sit and talk. A thousand years of Chinese occupation left their mark, however, and a more highbrow and formal tea culture evolved between the 13th and 15th centuries. The noble classes began using Chinese-style teapots and adopting a ceremonial approach to serving tea: drinking it was considered a refined and enlightened pursuit.

Tea wasn't grown commercially in Vietnam until the arrival of the French, who established the first tea gardens in Phu Tho province in 1890 and a tea research centre here in 1918, which is still in operation today.

TEA CULTIVATION

As tea prefers a cool climate with high humidity and rainfall, Vietnam's tea plantations are concentrated in the mountainous north and the central highlands. Here you'll find numerous smallholdings and large-scale tea plantations where tea bushes stretch as far as the eye can see; tea can also be found growing wild in Vietnam's upland forests.

Commercial plantations can yield up to six harvests in a single year (compared to four for wild tea), but though some 60% of the tea produced in Vietnam is black, green tea is the more popular variety among the Vietnamese. If you're after a Western-style cup of tea, you'll probably have to ask for a 'lip-ton' – a bag of the ubiquitous Lipton brand.

For the Vietnamese, everyday tea drinking is largely informal. In the humid south, a glass of iced green or jasmine tea is often served free at street food joints, or as a chaser after an iced coffee. In the north, which experiences a proper winter, hot green tea is the beverage of choice, usually drunk strong and bitter. Throughout the country, farmers, labourers, taxi drivers and street vendors will carry a flask of green tea to sip on during the day.

THE NGUYEN TEA CEREMONY

For Vietnamese connoisseurs, four words – *hòa* (peace), *kính* (respect for elders and friends), *thanh* (tranquillity) and *tich* (leisure) – are used to describe the poetry of tea drinking, a ritual which was first elevated to the status of art in Hue, imperial capital of the Nguyen Dynasty. According to the Hue custom, a 'tea course' was held for three people, who were seated around a three-sided traditional tea table set against a wall. The tea room would be intimate and tastefully decorated, although a tea course could also be held in a garden.

Pots and cups were selected according to the season, so that the patterns and design reflected or complemented the weather. Nguyen nobles used pots and cups with weighted, rounded bottoms that, if disturbed, would rock a bit and then right themselves – so symbolising the nation's ability to survive in spite of its historical ups and downs.

The other essentials for a traditional tea course were a charcoal brazier (with a few pieces of aromatic aquilaria wood to add to the coals), a boiling pot, an earthenware pot of cold water (usually rainwater or, on special occasions, dew gathered from lotus leaves), a

teapot, large and small teacups and a tea box. To make the tea, the host would boil the water then let it cool to about 90°C (194°F) before gently pouring it into the teapot, which was then covered tightly for about five minutes. During the steeping stage, tea-course etiquette demanded that guests comment on the design of the teapot or the fine aroma of the tea, and ensured that tea was kept as the focus of conversation. When ready, the tea was poured into a large cup known as the 'commander', from which it was then poured into smaller 'soldier' cups; this guaranteed even distribution of the tea's flavour and colour.

Though they probably won't involve lotus-leaf dew or priceless china, it's worth seeking out one of the tea houses in Hue, Hanoi and Dalat that still demonstrate this traditional tea ceremony for visitors.

TYPES OF TEA

As well as its fragrant, flower-scented teas, Vietnam produces five main types of tea from the leaves of the *camellia sinensis* plant.

BLACK TEA

(trà đen)

The most oxidised of the teas: the leaves are left to wither for an extended period, and then rolled to increase the rate of oxidation. During this process, new compounds are formed that change the leaf colour from green to dark brown, and produce stronger malt and chocolate flavours. The colour of the ready-to-drink leaves ranges from copper red to black.

DARK TEA

(trà phổ nhĩ)

Though Vietnam's ethnic minority groups have been making dark teas using wild-grown leaves for many years, commercial production only began recently. Similar in style to Chinese *pu-erh* teas, they resemble a sun-dried green tea but are processed to be suitable for long-term ageing, during which they develop distinct earthy, mineral flavours.

GREEN TEA

(trà xanh)

After picking, the leaves for green tea are heated to kill the enzymes that cause oxidation, which enables them to retain their green colour and their natural antioxidants. Green teas tend to be gentle and light, with grassy, floral, vegetable or toasty flavours

JASMINE TEA

(trà lài)

This is usually green tea, infused overnight with the scent of freshly opened jasmine blossoms.

UNUSUAL VIETNAMESE TEAS

LOTUS TEA

(trà sen)

The best lotus teas are made with lotus flowers picked at dawn before they open. The fine, powdery anthers are separated from the flowers by hand and blended with a suitable tea, a process that will be repeated seven times over a two week period before the final product is ready.

OOLONG TEA

(trà ô long)

Oolong teas sit in the middle of the oxidisation spectrum, being semi-oxidised at anywhere between 20% and 80%. Good oolongs are highly aromatic, with flavours ranging from floral to fruity to spicy; they vary in colour from yellow and green to deep amber.

WHITE TEA

(trà trắng)

The least processed of all teas, white varieties are often made from leaf buds only, via a simple but time-consuming process that generates more subtle, sweet and elegant flavours than in green tea. White tea usually has floral and fruity undertones, and is very pale yellow in colour.

ARTICHOKE TEA

(trà atisô)

The Vietnamese make two types of tea from the artichokes grown in the cool central highlands. The most common is a yellow tea made from the flowers, which has a delicate, nutty flavour and can be taken hot or cold. The intensely bitter black version is made from artichoke stems, and is considered detoxifying.

CHRYSANTHEMUM TEA

(trà hoa cúc)

Made from chrysanthemum flowers, this tea has a floral aroma and a light and slightly sweet flavour. According to traditional medicine, it's considered a cooling beverage.

GINGER TEA

(trà gừng)

This warming drink is considered a go-to when suffering from a cold or just feeling chilly.

VIETNAM'S MAGICAL, MIST-ICAL TEA

© Geoff Hopkins

© Geoff Hopkins

Above: Picking wild tea, Thông Nguyên
Left: *Trà shan tuyết* in bloom

Named for the fine white hairs that cover their leaves, *trà shan tuyết* or mountain snow tea comes from ancient trees, tended by H'mong and Dao minority families in the mist-shrouded mountains of northern Vietnam. Also referred to as wild tea, *trà shan tuyết* is associated with various superstitions: the Dao won't harvest the leaves on certain days, such as 'thunder day' (the first day of the third lunar month) and 'wind day'(the 20th day of the first lunar month), as any tea picked at these times will be ruined.

But thanks to the efforts of wholesale and retail tea business Hatvala ('bean and leaf' in Vietnamese), this ancient tea is experiencing something of a renaissance. Hatvala's owners, London-born Geoff Hopkins and Nguyen Thu Ngoc, who hails from the tea-growing province of Lao Cai, have become experts in *shan tuyết* tea. Although their business is based in Ho Chi Minh City, the couple are on a mission to discover new teas and further develop existing ones, and spend much of the year meeting,

Above: Green tea, served up in style with crystallised ginger

working with and drinking tea with local tea farmers in the mountains of northern Vietnam.

Many of Hatvala's signature teas are made with leaves harvested from wild tea trees, which have been left to grow naturally and organically in Vietnam's forests. 'The older trees are frequently found in mixed bio-diverse environments, often deep inside the forest and only accessible on foot', says Geoff Hopkins. 'When tea grows wild, you don't have problems with pests and with the soil being degraded. It's what being organic really should be about. There is simply no need to treat the plants with any chemicals.'

'Old trees with deep roots and slow growth give these wild mountain teas their special character which can be very different to farm-grown equivalents,' Hopkins continues. 'A wild tea may not have the same intensity of aroma as farmed varieties but it will continue to develop, have greater depth and complexity and deliver flavour for longer.'

Unsurprisingly, however, local officials have realised the economic potential of *shan tuyết* tea, and plans are afoot to expand the industry – and this may mean some tea labelled *shan tuyết* will actually come from farmed tea plants, rather than truly wild trees. Caveat emptor.

COFFEE

Vietnam is best-known for its slow-prep 'drip coffee', but the local coffee culture has been revitalised by a new generation of aficionados.

COFFEE CULTIVATION

Coffee plants were introduced to Vietnam's central highlands by French missionaries in 1857, and during the French colonial era, different varieties were tested throughout this lush, elevated part of the country. The coffee industry didn't grow much during the years of conflict with France and the US: according to the International Coffee Organization, Vietnam produced about 300,000 60kg (132lb) bags of coffee in 1986. Since then, however, coffee cultivation has expanded exponentially: today, Vietnam

© James Pham / Lonely Planet

Above: Coffee time in Ho Chi Minh City

© Lonely Planet

© Pramote Polyamate / Getty Images

© whitewish / Getty Images

Top: Coffee is an any-time drink in Vietnam
Bottom left: Arabica berries
Bottom right: *Cà phê sữa đá*

is the world's second-biggest producer after Brazil, churning out more than 25 million 60kg bags each year.

A ROBUSTA BREW

Although Vietnam's *cà phê sữa đá* (iced local-style filter coffee with condensed milk) has found international fame, Vietnamese coffee hasn't, mainly because the beans that the country exports are low quality and intended for processing into instant granules. About 97% of the coffee grown in Vietnam is the robusta variety, a high-yielding, pest-resistant strain that produces a bitter-tasting bean with a high caffeine content. The Vietnamese counter its bitterness by roasting the beans with 'butter oil', and serving it in various ways that enhance other flavours. Most of the coffee sold in Vietnam is a coarsely ground, dark roast which, as well as being used in the ubiquitous *phin* one-cup filters, works well in a French press or in drip-filter coffee machines.

AN INDUSTRY ON THE UP

Vietnam's coffee industry is on the cusp of modernisation. Much of the country's coffee is grown by subsistence farmers using the traditional methods of strip-picking ripe and unripe cherries (as the beans are called) and then drying them, unsorted, on a plastic tarpaulin. This practice relies heavily on good weather, and on a slow and long roasting process to create beans of a uniform colour. As a result, many farmers are expanding their production of arabica beans, experimenting with new varieties such as yellow bourbon, typica and geisha, and modernising their drying and roasting methods.

CAFÉ SOCIETY

For the Vietnamese, a coffee is something to be enjoyed at leisure – the polar opposite of the Italian espresso, which is thrown down in one gulp. The savouring of coffee is often a social experience, hence Vietnam's thriving café culture, which centres around the languid appreciation of a *cà phê phin*: fresh ground coffee dripped slowly through a cup-top metal filter into a glass, often called 'drip coffee' in English.

Whether they're on a sidewalk or in a hammock-strewn garden, or belong to the modern new breed of

© James Pham/Lonely Planet

© James Pham/Lonely Planet

Above: Streetside coffee stall

Courtesy of The Workshop

Above: Instagram-friendly café culture in Ho Chi Minh City

Above: The Workshop specialises in artisan coffees

Instagram-worthy air-con indoor places, cafés are an integral part of Vietnamese life. As well as being places to gather for a chat and a coffee, they offer young people living in multigenerational homes a little privacy, a place to meet in groups without the pressure of a formal 'date', to do homework or just use the wi-fi for gaming and watching movies on a laptop (not necessarily using earphones). Cafés are also much-used for business meetings and remote work.

THE VARIATIONS OF *CÀ PHÊ PHIN*

One of the most popular *phin*-filtered brews is the black coffee and condensed milk brew that's referred to as *cà phê nâu* (brown coffee) in the north, and *cà phê sữa* (milk coffee) in the south; wherever you drink it, the preparation ritual adds to the leisurely experience.

The basic setup involves a one-cup phin filter, which sits atop a short glass with a dollop of condensed milk at the bottom. Very slowly, the hot water drips through the *phin* into the glass, creating mesmerising swirls as the black coffee mixes with the milk, and giving the drinker time to sit back and relax. Once the *phin* is empty, its lid is flipped over to serve as a saucer, and the coffee and milk are mixed. For the *cà phê sữa đá* version (literally 'coffee-milk-ice', a mainly southern preference), the hot coffee is tipped into a long ice-filled glass; there might be a separate bowl of ice and some tongs north of Ho Chi Minh City, but there's always a long-stemmed spoon to give it a final mix and distribute the coffee through the ice. The result is a smooth, creamy, sweet and chocolatey iced coffee.

Throughout the central highlands, coffee is served warm, in shot glasses, and has the consistency of motor oil. It's easy to down it in one go, but this type of coffee, too, is designed to be savoured. Unsurprisingly, hot coffee is the drink of choice in the cool north.

© Anup Shah / Getty Images

Above: Civets pay a high price for the world's most expensive coffee

CIVET COFFEE

The Vietnamese origins of this famously unusual – and famously expensive – coffee are somewhat hazy. One version has it that, during their hundred-year rule of Vietnam, the French wouldn't allow local farmers to drink the coffee they were cultivating. The farmers, too, were dealing with the night-time raids of the omnivorous native Asian palm civet, which had discovered that the berries of this newly imported plant were an easy snack. Noticing that the civet scat was full of the banned beans (civets can't digest the hard bean within the soft exterior of the fruit, and excrete them whole), some curious farmer decided to wash them out of the scat and brew up some illicit coffee.

Soon everyone was doing it, and when the Indonesian version, kopi luwak, *caught international attention, Vietnamese coffee farmers stepped up the marketing of this unique product, known here as* cà phê chồn. *Thanks to the enzymes in the civet's digestive system, which partially ferment the bean and reduce its bitterness, civet coffee has become highly prized – it's said to be smooth and buttery, often with chocolate notes.*

However, the demand for civet coffee has led to battery farming of the animal, which is naturally a solitary creature and suffers greatly from being kept in captivity, in close proximity to others. Quite apart from the ethical considerations, the coffee itself is so prohibitively expensive that most visitors wouldn't consider buying it; bear in mind, too, that visiting a plantation which advertises cà phê chồn *endorses this cruelty, and is not advised. It is possible to sample a similarly treated Vietnamese coffee, however. In 1996, Vietnamese coffeemaker Trung Nguyen asked a group of German scientists to replicate the civet's digestive enzyme, and his Legendee coffee is made using a natural enzyme-soak process that doesn't involve any animals.*

Courtesy of The Wrokshop

Above: Indulge in bean-to-cup coffee concoctions at The Workshop

VIETNAMESE COFFEE CULTURE

There's a new wave of coffee appreciation in Vietnam, which loosely divides into two branches. The first is the more superficial: pretty drinks and fancy decor to appeal to the Instagram generation. Places of this ilk can be a lot of fun, especially when you discover hidden cafés tucked away down dingy alleys or up dark flights of crumbling staircases. They also offer the chance to sample uniquely Vietnamese concoctions like yoghurt coffee, avocado coffee, coconut coffee and egg coffee (originally a Hanoi speciality but now found outside the capital).

The second branch of Vietnam's coffee revolution is focused on the appreciation of, and experimentation with, all things coffee-related. Local farmers are planting new varieties of coffee and trialling innovative roasting techniques, and some have started small cooperatives to make and market their beans. Formed by K'ho ethnic minority families from Lang Biang in the central highlands, K'ho Coffee focuses on organic cultivation of heirloom arabica strains (typica, bourbon, yellow bourbon and a catura hybrid), and on craft fermentation techniques. Their beans are used by cafés in Dalat, Ho Chi Minh City, Hanoi, Nha Trang, Hoi An and Mui Ne, and sold at the co-op farm shop and through their website.

Specialist cafés are also promoting this new wave of coffee appreciation by experimenting with unusual preparation techniques, from cold-filter and pour-over methods to siphon machines and cold-brew coffee infused with nitrogen. Cafés such as The Workshop, a hard-to-find gem in downtown Ho Chi Minh City, have a bean-to-cup approach, displaying photos of the farmer who grew the beans for their coffee of the day, and trialling blends of local and imported beans; they also run regular coffee appreciation workshops. Over in Hanoi, Atelier Coffee Roaster focuses on 'fine' robusta beans prepared in a variety of ways; as well as espresso, Americano and latte, there's *hatsukoi*, made with steamed milk, salt, pepper and cinnamon.

SMOOTHIES, JUICE, MILK AND SOFT DRINKS

Sipping on the water from a fresh coconut (*dừa tươi*) is virtually compulsory while in Vietnam, and there are plenty of other delicious non-alcoholic alternatives, too, many based on fresh local fruit.

SMOOTHIES AND FRUIT JUICES

Smoothies and juice are often super-sweet, thanks to liberal amounts of added sugar or, as in smoothies, a generous dollop of sweetened condensed milk along with the fruit and ice. Be aware, too, that drinks listed as a juice may be made from a concentrated fruit cordial – there's usually no way of knowing until you take a sip. Smoothie ingredients and juices vary according to seasonal availability; keep an eye out for soursop and avocado versions, and try a durian smoothie if you dare. There's some regional variation, too: cold-climate Dalat is known for its strawberry smoothies.

Above: Ice-cold watermelon juice

© Jasmin Krpan / Alamy Stock Photo

Left: *Nước mía* sugar-cane juice is a popular street drink

NƯỚC MÍA

The Vietnamese have a sweet tooth when it comes to drinks, and though sugar-cane juice (*nước mía*) sounds like it might be the sweetest of the lot, it's saved from syrupiness by the addition of some tart kumquat. A popular street drink, *nước mía* is sold from little carts on every second street corner, advertised by sticks of sugar-cane sitting in a bucket in front of the stall itself, which doubles up as a hand-operated machine for extracting the juice from the cane. It works something like an old-fashioned mangle: a stalk of sugar-cane and a couple of kumquats are pushed through the rollers, which are turned by a wheel, and the juice is collected at the bottom. The astringent kumquat balances the sweetness of the sugar-cane to create a very refreshing drink; thanks to its quotient of antioxidants, calcium, magnesium, potassium and iron, *nước mía* is considered to be a healthy option by the Vietnamese.

© Mauro Ladu / Alamy Stock Photo

Above: You're never far from a cold drink in Vietnam

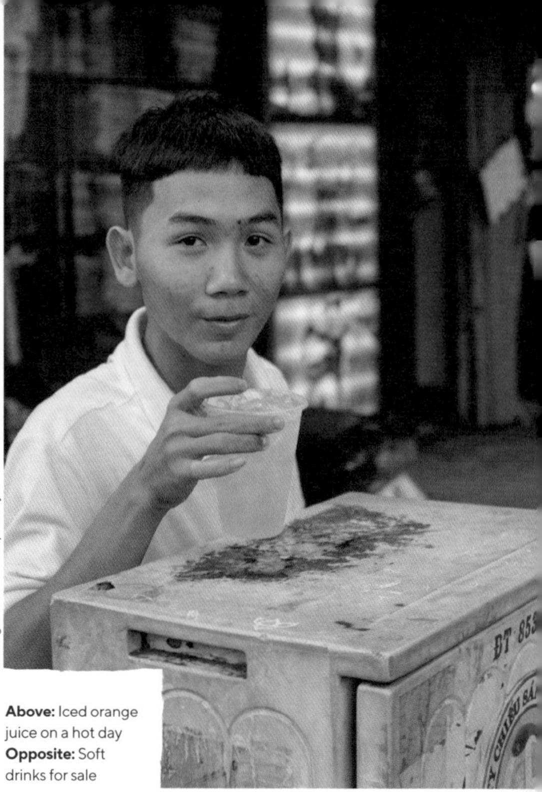

© Angus MacKinnon / Alamy Stock Photo

Above: Iced orange juice on a hot day
Opposite: Soft drinks for sale

SODA CHANH

Pronounced 'so-dah-chan', with each syllable given equal emphasis, *soda chanh* is a refreshing pick-me-up on a hot day, made with soda water, a squeeze of lime and a fair bit of sugar – you can ask for 'không đường' (no sugar) or 'ít đường' (a little sugar). Even though this drink sounds simple enough, it can get quite complicated in some places if the components are served separately for a DIY version.

MILK AND YOGHURT DRINKS

Fresh milk is available in Vietnam, but UHT is usually the local preference; it's sold in bags, and in single-serve or 1L boxes. When buying plain milk, make sure you read the fine print, as there are two varieties: *có đường* (with sugar) and *không đường* (no sugar). Outside of the major tourist centres, *có đường* is often the only milk available, so you might want to stock up beforehand if heading into the countryside.

Packaged yoghurt drinks are also available in supermarkets and corner stores, either in tiny containers (such as Yakult), larger single-serve boxes or even 750mL bottles. You'll sometimes see a page of yoghurt options on a restaurant's drinks menu; these are usually not drinks, but small bowls of yoghurt and fruit.

IS THE ICE OK?

Usually – yes. A relic of the French era, the hundreds of ice factories dotted around Vietnam are the source of most of the ice used by drinks vendors. Recognisable by its machine-made look (usually cubes or cylinders), this is generally a no-risk addition to your cold drink or coffee. Think twice about crushed ice, which is made by hand, or irregularly shaped shards that may have been chipped from a home-made block.

REGIONAL SPECIALITIES

Black sesame milk (sữa hạt mè đen) *A Dalat speciality, this is a warm drink made with a blend of black sesame seeds and sweet soy milk; find it (alongside peanut milk) at the hole-in-the-wall Hoa Sữa soy shop, on Dalat's Tang Bat Ho Street.*

Egg coffee (cà phê trứng) *This custardy, dessert-like take on coffee was first served at Café Giang in Hanoi's Old Quarter in the 1940s, and is now fairly widely available in Hanoi and Ho Chi Minh City. Egg yolks and condensed milk are beaten together until light and fluffy, then poured over hot coffee.*

Herbal tea (nước sâm) *Usually served iced, this sweet, nutty and cooling 'tea' from Ho Chi Minh City has varying recipes that can include sugar cane, nettle leaves, corn silk, grass roots, roasted water chestnuts and chrysanthemum.*

Lime tea (trà chanh) *A refreshing Hanoi-style street drink of sweetened green tea and lime juice, served iced with a slice of lime.*

Mulberry juice (nước ép dâu tằm) *Dalat mulberries are made into a sweet syrup that forms the basis of this cooling summer drink. The town's locally grown strawberries, however, are used fresh to make a popular strawberry smoothie.*

Peanut milk (sữa đậu nành) *Another Dalat speciality: toasted peanuts are blended and then boiled with sweetened pandan-flavoured soy milk. Order it alongside the little local pastries and dunk them in the warm drink.*

Pennywort or gotu kola juice (nước rau má) *Made from the* centella asiatica *plant, this Ho Chi Minh City speciality is the Vietnamese equivalent of wheatgrass juice, taken for its medicinal and detoxifying benefits; fresh leaves are usually blended with mung beans or coconut water.*

SOFT DRINKS AND SODAS

Alongside the usual gamut of fizzy drinks, from Coca-Cola ('coca' to the Vietnamese) to 7-Up, less well-known options include Teppy (an orange juice drink), Nutriboost (a milk and juice concoction), Marinda (orange soda), Tea-Plus (bottled oolong tea), Sting (an energy drink with caffeine, ginseng and B vitamins) and Revive (an isotonic drink). There are also some Vietnamese carbonated drinks, such as Sá Xị Chương Dương (sarsaparilla/root beer), alongside a host of canned and plastic-bottled beverages that promise all kinds of health benefits, such as Nước Yến (bird's nest drink) and Dr Thanh (herbal tea).

© John Seaton Callahan / Getty Images

BEER

From a kerbside *bia hơi* to a glass of craft ale served at an artisan brewery, beer is big business in Vietnam.

VIETNAMESE BEER CULTURE

Beer is very popular in Vietnam, and though drinking has traditionally been perceived as a mostly male activity, this is changing, with groups of young women starting to frequent the country's bars.

Drinking here is a social activity that usually involves food and a fair bit of noise. If you're invited to *đi nhậu* (go drinking), you'll be expected to keep up with your co-drinkers – in Vietnam, every sip is toasted, so you drink at the pace of the thirstiest person in the group. The basic toast, which gets louder as a *đi nhậu* session progresses, is a very simple 'một, hai, ba, vô' ('one, two, three – drink!'); the *vô* is pronounced 'yo' in the south, 'zho' in the north. The question of what is toasted? It's a broad church. It might be good news of any kind, birthdays, jokes, sports results, a new arrival to the table, the confused face of a foreigner. *Vô!* Take a sip. Someone forgets to *vô* ... *Vô!* Take a sip.

Bear in mind, too, that there are regional variations in beer drinking habits. In northern Hanoi, there's no ice in the beer; down in Ho Chi Minh City in the sultry south, a giant cylinder of ice in your beer glass is standard.

DRINKING ETIQUETTE

Even though Vietnamese drinking sessions appear very informal, there is a bit of etiquette involved. First, if you're invited to go drinking, whoever issued the invitation will order the food and pay the bill. Offering to contribute or even trying to see the bill can be considered offensive, though you can ask the host to order a dish that takes your fancy. Splitting a drinking bill usually only happens within a group of close friends.

There's also a slight air of competitiveness when it comes to drinking, with the empty bottles kept with the group under the table, or in a crate beside, as the night progresses. Vietnamese drinkers regard a lot of empty bottles as a sign of strength, and there is some status attached to various brands – Heineken is considered a 'high class' beer.

As faces get redder and voices louder, challenges are issued. One drinker will point to another and say 'một trăm phần trăm' ('100%'); both drinkers are then expected to down everything in their glass. You can try to negotiate the amount by countering with 'năm mươi phần trăm' ('50%'), but this will probably lead to a bit of teasing banter.

Above: Bia Hanoi, served chilled or southern Vietnam-style over ice

At a certain point, someone might claim to be too full to stomach any more beer. But that doesn't mean they're going to stop drinking; instead, it usually indicates they're going to add some hard stuff into the mix. A bottle of scotch, vodka or rice wine will appear, along with a shot glass, and whoever ordered the bottle will be in charge of its dispersal. In the same manner as the 100% challenge, they will nominate another drinker to take an obligatory shot; sometimes close friends share one shot glass, drinking half each. With colleagues and acquaintances, there will be more than one glass, so everyone involved downs a full shot. And even as the shots are being dispensed, everyone is simultaneously drinking beer and *vô*-ing.

DRINK-DRIVING LAWS

The Vietnamese government's introduction of strict new drink-driving laws in early 2020 caused an instant slump in the number of people going out drinking, and an estimated 25% drop in beer sales. Motorbike riders caught with any trace of alcohol on their breath now face licence suspensions of up to two years, and fines that equate to more than double the average monthly wage of many Vietnamese (around US$345); car and truck drivers caught under the influence face fines of up to US$1726. The intention is clear: designate a driver.

© Ville Palonen / Alamy Stock Photo

Above: Fresh-brewed *bia hơi* is an essential Vietnamese tipple

REGIONAL VIETNAMESE BEERS

The most popular international beer brands are Heineken and Tiger, but there are also several home-grown beers with dedicated followings; none are going to win any international plaudits, but all are eminently drinkable in Vietnam's sultry climate. Although most are available throughout the country these days, the Vietnamese tend to have a strong preference for their local lager; the beers below are listed alphabetically.

333

This popular, straw-coloured Ho Chi Minh City lager has been around since the late 1800s. In the 1970s, an extra three was added to the name of what locals call 'ba-ba-ba' (333).

BIA HANOI

A pale lager produced in Hanoi by Habeco (Hanoi Beer, Alcohol, Beverage Joint Stock Corporation), established by Frenchman Alfred Hommel in 1890, and government-owned since the 1950s.

BIERE LARUE

Most popular in Hoi An and southern regions, this crisp, hoppy beer was first brewed in 1909 by Frenchman Victor Larue, who founded Glacieres Brasseries d'Indochine in 1875. A favourite of American troops in Vietnam during the war, it was known as Tiger Beer for the tiger logo on its label. It's now made by Heineken, which has six breweries in Vietnam.

ĐẠI VIỆT

Available as a lager or a dark beer, and brewed in Hanoi by Huong Sen Group.

HALIDA

One of the cheapest lagers in the market, Halida is brewed in northern Vietnam by the Danish giant Carlsberg. The name is abbreviation of Hanoi, liên doanh ('joint venture' in Vietnamese) and Đan Mạch (Denmark in Vietnamese).

HUDA

Brewed by Carlsberg in Hue, the name of this pilsner-style beer combines Hue and Đan Mạch (Denmark).

SAIGON GREEN, RED & SPECIAL

These three decent lagers are brewed in Ho Chi Minh City by Sabeco (formerly the Southern Beer and Alcohol Company, now known as the Saigon Beer and Beverage Joint Stock Company); the green variety is the best of the bunch.

TRUC BACH BEER

Another pale Habeco lager, named after Hanoi's Truc Bach Lake.

ZOROK

Brewed in the Binh Duong province near Ho Chi Minh City by SABMiller Vietnam, this beer has not found much success with locals. What might seem a groovy name to an English speaker is very difficult to pronounce here, as the Vietnamese alphabet doesn't have a Z.

© dave stamboulis / Alamy Stock Photo

BIA HỞI

A streetside bia hởi *('fresh beer') is almost compulsory for visitors to Hanoi; the best place to drink a few are the bars crowding the intersection of Ta Hien and Luong Ngoc Quyen in the capital's Old Quarter. This home-brewed draft beer contains no preservatives (it must be drunk within 24 hours of being made), and has a lower alcohol content than most beers produced commercially in Vietnam.* Bia hởi *bars are typically outside affairs, with small plastic stools spilling out onto the pavements, and beer served in the distinctively rough, slightly bluish* cốc vại *glasses created by Vietnamese designer Le Huy Van in 1976, and still made in the Nam Dinh village of Xoi Tri from recycled glass.*

CRAFT BEER

Below: Pasteur Street Brewing Company's pale ale

Vietnam is in the grip of a craft beer craze. Ho Chi Minh City's Pasteur Street Brewing Company launched its first artisan brew in 2015, and today, craft beer is a nationwide phenomenon that's popular with locals, expats and tourists.

Courtesy of Pasteur Street Brewing Co.

MICROBREWS TO CRAFT BEER

Before today's craft beer specialists appeared, there were several microbreweries operating in Vietnam, mostly using Czech brewing techniques. The best-known of these is Hoa Vien Brauhaus, which opened in Ho Chi Minh City in 2001 and now has five outlets, including two in Hanoi; most popular choices are their pilsner and dark beers.

Set up by two American expats, the Pasteur Street Brewing Company kicked off Vietnam's craft beer scene, serving their first brew in 2015 at their Ho Chi Minh City District 1 taproom. The company's aim was to marry American craft brewing techniques with Vietnamese flavours such as jasmine, ginger, lemongrass and cinnamon – their Cyclo Imperial Chocolate Stout won a gold medal at the World Beer Cup in 2016, while other favourites include the God Water beer, made with a dash of Phu Quoc black pepper; the Passionfruit Wheat Ale, with a good balance of sweet and tart; and the Dragon Fruit Gose, with sour and salty notes and a pretty pink hue. The business has expanded swiftly, with several new taprooms in Ho Chi Minh City, as well as outlets in Hanoi and Hoi An.

© Charlise Ha - Chau Ha / Lonely Planet

Above: Pasteur Street's District 1 taproom, Ho Chi Minh City

With a taproom in Ho Chi Minh City, Heart of Darkness produce a range of craft beers with typically esoteric names, such as the malty and refreshing Futile Purpose Cucumber Pilsner or the creamy, full-bodied Excited Magpie Dry Irish Stout. Their brews have also picked up international awards, and are available canned at bars in most of Vietnam's larger cities. Look out, too, for offerings from other Ho Chi Minh City breweries: East West Brewing, Winking Seal, Te Te and Belgo.

The craft beer scene isn't limited to HCMC, however. In Hanoi, the major artisan brewer is Furbrew, which makes the phở-flavoured Bia Phở, a deliciously sweet, spicy, umami-rich concoction; this and other Furbrew beers are available at their own taproom and at eateries around Hanoi. In Danang, the local craft outfit is 7 Bridges Brewing Company, a socially conscious enterprise with its own taproom overlooking the Dragon Bridge; look out for their fruity Vietnam Red Ale, and the floral notes of Sunset Tangerine wheat beer.

CIDER

There is a small craft cider industry in Vietnam, led by expats who turned a hobby into beer-alternative businesses. Saigon Cider took home a fistful of medals at the 2019 Asia Beer Championship, including the Chairman's Choice award for its apple and ginger cider; they also claim to have made the world's first chilli cider. Hanoi Cider, meanwhile, dabbles in local fruits and natural flavourings, creating mulberry, mango and lemongrass-ginger ciders, and has a taproom and restaurant, Hanoi Cider House, in the capital's Tay Ho district.

© Peter Stuckings / Getty Images

Above: Harvesting rice, the essential ingredient of fiery *rượu*

RƯỢU

Just as the Vietnamese language uses the same word, *chuột*, for mouse and rat, the word *rượu* covers grape-based wine as well as all kinds of fiery liquor distilled from rice and corn.

RICE WINE

Rice wine has been brewed in Vietnam for centuries, and though it's considered an old person's drink these days, there are still several large-scale producers and a host of regional specialities. The name is something of a misnomer: this is not so much a wine as a spirit, with an alcohol volume that ranges from 20% to 50% – it can pack quite a punch. Beware, too, of drinking home-made rice wine. Every year the Vietnamese media carries reports of people falling ill or even dying after drinking 'fake' rice wine made with industrial-grade methanol – stick to mass-produced brands rather than something out of a repurposed mineral water bottle.

RICE WINE COMES IN SEVERAL FORMS, THE MOST COMMON OF WHICH ARE:

STICKY RICE WINE

(rượu nếp)

Made from fermented sticky rice, this is a clear, sweetish liquor; *rượu nếp cẩm*, made from black sticky rice, is dark red.

© agefotostock / Alamy Stock Photo

TUBE WINE

(rượu cần)

This is a communal 'party' wine that's popular in the central highlands. It can be distilled from rice, cassava, sweet potato or corn, and enhanced with a variety of herbs. It's made in large ceramic pots – when it's party time, long reed straws (the tubes for which this drink is named) are poked through the pot's cover into the liquor below. Everyone takes turns to suck on the straws, and when the pot appears to be running low it's topped up with water to extend the drinking session.

MEDICINE WINE

(rượu thuốc)

The base starch used to make *rượu thuốc* comes second to the various additions, which are believed to have medicinal value. Of the 200-plus varieties of *rượu thuốc*, several contain whole animals or animal parts; mostly, though, they're infused with herbs and fruits. *Rượu chuối* (banana wine) is considered good for the skin, digestion, back pain and kidney stones, while *rượu mật ong* (honey wine) is said to improve metabolism, detoxify and boost the immune system.

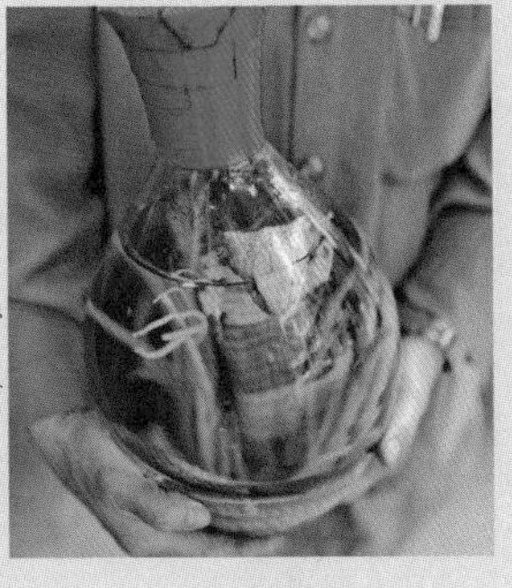

© Ville Palonen / Alamy Stock Photo

ANIMAL WINES

*The Vietnamese government has outlawed snake wine (*rượu rắn*), rice wine with snake parts or a whole snake infused into the alcohol. More widely, it's also illegal to buy, catch or consume endangered animals in Vietnam (the penalty for doing so is up to 15 years in prison), so do not buy or consume any 'aphrodisiac' rice wines containing snakes, seahorses, starfish, tiger bones or bear parts; and to be on the safe side, avoid* rượu thuốc *(medicinal wine) that contains lizards, scorpions or birds. If you're inclined to try* rượu thuốc*, go for a herb or fruit variety.*

© PRADEEP RAJA KANNAIAH / Alamy Stock Photo

REGIONAL RƯỢU SPECIALITIES

RƯỢU BÀU ĐÁ

Hailing from south-central Binh Dinh, this is a clear, rice-based wine made with water from an ancient spring in Cu Lam village. The ABV can be as high as 50%.

RƯỢU CẦN Ê ĐÊ BAN MÊ

A honey coloured sticky-rice wine from Dak Lak province in the central highlands, made with galangal and liquorice root.

RƯỢU KIM SƠN

A sticky-rice wine from Ninh Binh province in the Red River Delta, made with traditional medicinal herbs and well water.

RƯỢU LÀNG VÂN

Made in northeast Vietnam's Bac Giang province, using glutinous or sticky rice and Chinese herbs.

RƯỢU MẪU SƠN

Usually made by Dao families in the northern province of Lang Son using rice, spring water and herbs harvested from the jungle.

RƯỢU NGÔ MEN LÁ NA HANG

Corn-based, herb-infused wine from northeast Vietnam.

RƯỢU NGÔ

A speciality of minority groups from northeast Bac Ha province, distilled from corn and with a sweet and mild flavour.

RƯỢU PHÚ LỄ

This brown-rice and well-water Mekong Delta wine is buried for 100 days to absorb the yin and yang of heaven and earth.

RƯỢU SIM

A speciality of Phu Quoc island, made with rose myrtle fruit; the good stuff tastes like a fortified blackberry wine.

Opposite: Traditional *rượu* distillery
Below: Cardinal grapes on the vine at Phan Rang

© NgKhanhVuKhoa / Getty Images

WINE

Young professionals are driving an increasing demand for grape-based wine in Vietnam: fancy wine bars are popping up in the bigger cities, and wines from France, Italy, Spain, Chile, Australia and New Zealand are available at restaurants and specialist wine shops throughout the country. The high import taxes mean you'll pay more for them than you would at home, although a trade agreement between Vietnam and Chile means that Chilean wine attracts less tax.

Vietnam also produces wine, though it gets mixed reviews. The main brand is Vang Đà Lạt, which makes reds and whites from a blend of fermented mulberry juice and cardinal grapes from nearby Phan Rang. The bitterness of the cardinal variety, which is mainly used for table grapes and raisins in other countries, comes through in the wine, which can be up to 16% ABV. The Passion brand of wines are labelled as a 'wine of Chile', but are a local product nonetheless, and tend to be slightly more drinkable than Dalat wine.

Left: Nam Dinh in northern Vietnam during the Tran Temple Festival

REGIONAL CUISINE

Vietnamese cuisine is usually classified by geography, with fairly distinct cooking styles in each of the country's three main regions: northern, central and southern Vietnam. There are many variations within these areas, and throughout the country, Vietnamese people eat what's in season wherever they are, whether it's seafood from the ocean or ant eggs from the forest.

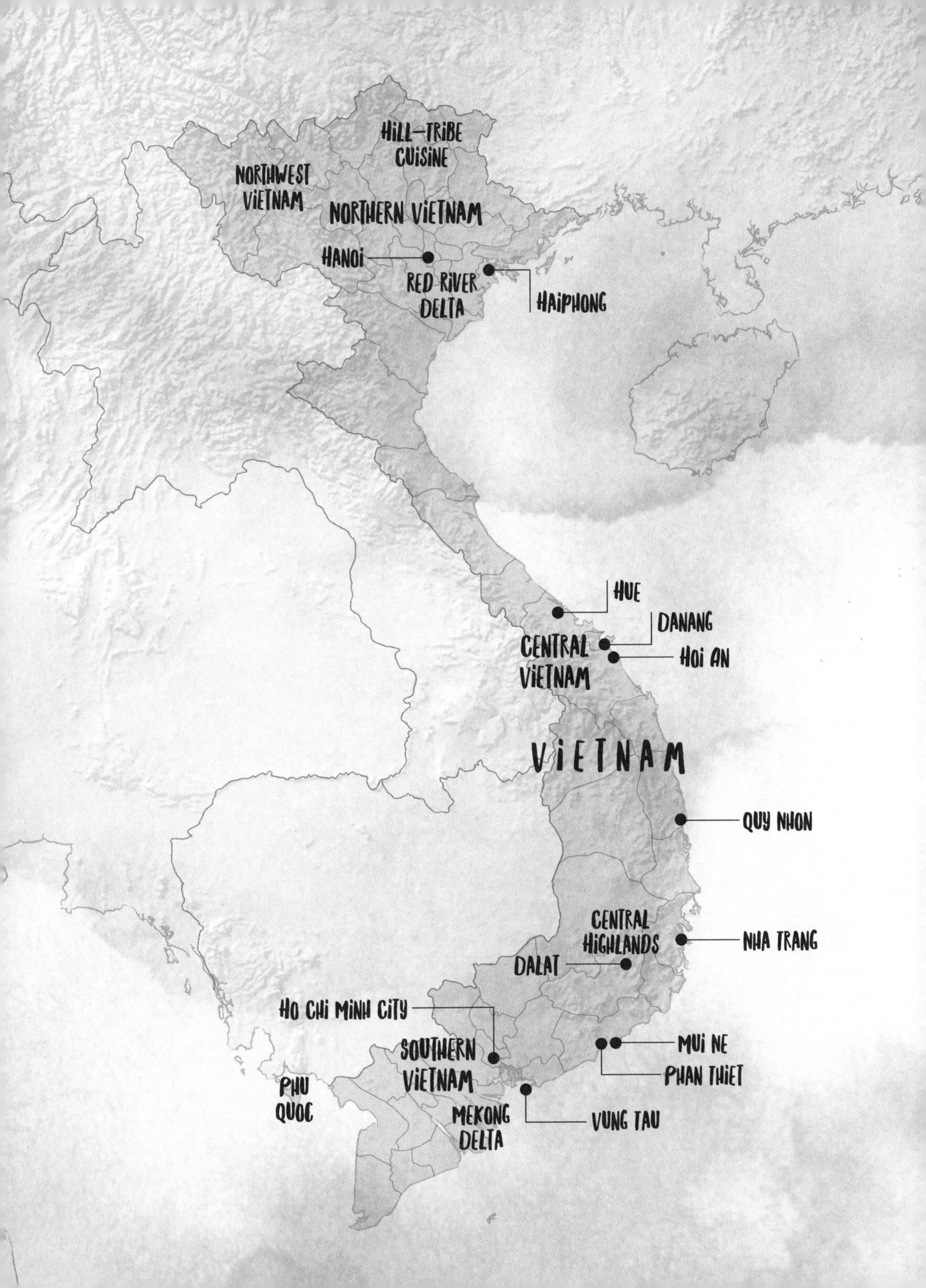
HILL-TRIBE CUISINE
NORTHWEST VIETNAM
NORTHERN VIETNAM
HANOI
RED RIVER DELTA
HAIPHONG
HUE
DANANG
CENTRAL VIETNAM
HOI AN
VIETNAM
QUY NHON
CENTRAL HIGHLANDS
NHA TRANG
DALAT
HO CHI MINH CITY
MUI NE
SOUTHERN VIETNAM
PHAN THIET
PHU QUOC
VUNG TAU
MEKONG DELTA

THE NORTH

Of all the country's cooking styles, northern cuisine is the most heavily influenced by China, Vietnam's big northern neighbour and one-time ruler. The food of the north is considered light, clean and balanced, and employs much more black pepper than in other areas. Because northern Vietnam experiences four seasons, and so has limited windows for cultivation, herbs and vegetables are used less liberally than in other areas of the country. Northerners also like sour flavours, with limes and pickled vegetables used to complement meals.

In the mountainous northwest subregion, ethnic minority groups still live in self-sufficient villages and the food is simple, relying on seasonal harvests and what can be hunted and gathered from the forests. In visitor-friendly Sapa, the northwest's most accessible town, local fare is available as street food or from rustic little restaurants. Hill tribes also live in the mountain areas of the northeast subregion, which includes the fertile Red River Delta, the fisheries of the Gulf of Tonkin and the cities of Hanoi and Haiphong, both with alluring foodie scenes.

CENTRAL VIETNAM

Central Vietnam includes the former imperial capital of Hue and the quaint former port of Hoi An. The weather is hot and the coastline is long, and the central region is known for its strong, bold flavours, for spicy dishes, seafood and the decorative and complex small dishes of imperial cuisine. The chefs of central Vietnam place strong emphasis on the visual appeal of a dish, with a preference for red and dark brown colours. And, like the food in the north, the specialities of central Vietnam also feature a lot of fermented fish products. As well as the north-central subregion around Hue, the area's south-central coast offers fabulous seafood in Danang, Hoi An, Quy Nhon, Nha Trang and Mui Ne. Up in the cool and misty central highlands,

THE SPREAD OF SOUTHERN CUISINE

What the rest of the world considers to be Vietnamese food is essentially southern Vietnamese cuisine, for it was southerners who fled the country at the end of the American War and during the Communist era in the late 1970s and early '80s. These refugees couldn't take much to their new homes around the world, but they did bring their recipes and their taste preferences: for sweet and sour flavours, fresh herbs and lots of spices.

However, Vietnamese cuisine is not just southern cuisine. As well as the three main regional cuisines, there are innumerable local specialities, some specific to one town, some specific to one of Vietnam's 63 provinces. There are also many regional nuances to dishes that are available throughout the country.

there's more fine Vietnamese cooking in quirky Dalat, a former French hill station once known as Le Petit Paris.

© ImaginativeGifts / Shutterstock

Above: A slow paddle through the Mekong Delta waterways

SOUTHERN VIETNAM AND THE MEKONG DELTA

Encompassing Ho Chi Minh City, the fertile Mekong Delta and the beautiful islands of Con Dao and Phu Quoc, southern Vietnam has the country's most obviously tropical climate, with a long rainy season lasting from May to November. Fresh herbs, rice, fruit and vegetables grow in abundance, and are integral to the food here. Southern cuisine is known for being sweeter than in other parts of the country, with sugar a key ingredient in clay-pot dishes and even in some soups. International influences are also more noticeable, from French to Cantonese, Khmer and Thai ingredients and techniques.

SAME DISH, DIFFERENT NAME

Throughout Vietnam, you'll encounter different versions of the very same dish, and these variations are usually identified by the town or region from which the dish originated. A classic example is hủ tiếu *noodle soup, considered a southern dish but also common in the south-central coastal areas – in Ho Chi Minh City, the most common version is* hủ tiếu Nam Vang *(Phnom Penh-style; Nam Vang is the old Vietnamese name for the Cambodian capital); you may also see* hủ tiếu Mỹ Tho *and* hủ tiếu Sa Đéc, *named (respectively) for the Mekong Delta towns of Mỹ Tho and Sa Đéc. And to add to the complexity, dishes are also sometimes named for their ingredients: the everyday version of* hủ tiếu *contains pork, prawns and quail's eggs – but* hủ tiếu mực *is made with* mực *(squid), and* hủ tiếu sa tế *is a spicy version laced with the chilli-and-lemongrass* sa tế *condiment. Ironically, even with all the different versions found in Vietnam and Cambodia,* hủ tiếu *is originally a Teochew dish, brought to southern Vietnam from China's Guangdong province by migrants about 300 years ago.*

NORTHERN VIETNAM

The cradle of both Vietnamese civilisation and of the country's thousand-year occupation by the Chinese, northern Vietnam has an austere regional cuisine that's heavily influenced by its northern neighbour. Most dishes are light and subtle, with flavours centred on one main ingredient.

© Vietnam Stock Images / Shutterstock

Above: Grilled meats are a northern speciality

CLIMATIC CUISINE

Northern Vietnamese food bears the imprint of centuries of Chinese occupation. Comforting noodle dishes, mild flavours and rustic elegance underpin the region's cuisine. Soy is used as frequently as fish sauce, vinegar rather than lime juice or tamarind is used to add sourness, black pepper takes over from chillies, and slow cooking coaxes maximum flavour from unpretentious ingredients.

With four distinct seasons, and snow often dusting the highest peaks during winter, the climate of northern Vietnam has also had a huge impact on the area's cuisine. Cold weather means warming meals: soups and fried food, laced with pepper and ginger. And those living in the harsher rural areas survive the winter by relying on preserved food, either fermented, dried or smoked.

Above: Lung Cu flag tower, marking Vietnam's northernmost point

In the north, as is the case throughout Vietnam, most meals revolve around rice in its many forms, whether it's simply boiled rice *(cơm)*, rice-flour noodles or a few shots of rice wine to wash everything down. Plain rice can be topped with meat or seafood, depending on the proximity of the river or ocean, and noodles can be prepared 'dry' or 'wet' as a soup. Whether farmed or foraged, local vegetables also form part of every meal, though perhaps in less lavish proportions than down south.

The foodie centres of northern cuisine are Hanoi and Haiphong, prosperous cities surrounded by the fertile plains of the Red River Delta, and with easy access to the bounty of rivers, streams and the Gulf of Tonkin, which includes the Unesco-listed Halong Bay. Life is much harder in the mountains, with extreme weather and landscapes that are dramatically beautiful but hard to cultivate. The resident hill tribe communities rely on subsistence farming, and enjoy simple food prepared with local, seasonal ingredients. Sapa is the main tourist destination in the northern mountains; foodie highlights here include the specialities of the area's ethnic minorities, from grilled skewers of meat and vegetables to *cơm lam* (bamboo rice).

NORTHWEST VIETNAM

Bordering China and Laos, Vietnam's remote, mountainous and ruggedly beautiful northwest includes the provinces of Dien Bien, Hoa Binh, Lai Chau, Lao Cai, Son La and Yen Bai. More than 20 ethnic minority groups live here, most with their own languages, festivals, customs and, of course, food.

NORTHWEST CUISINE

The food of northwest Vietnam is generally simple farmer's fare – *cơm lam* (bamboo rice), *gà nướng* (grilled chicken) and *thịt lợn xiên nướng* (pork skewers) are staples. The area's challenging geography and climate mean that anything that is edible will be eaten, including ant eggs, moth larvae and cicadas. *Ve sầu chiên* (fried cicadas) are more easily found in the summer months, when the insects shed their skins. From December to February, Dien Bien and Lai Châu locals harvest *sâu chít,* the larvae of the crambid moth, which is used in porridge and omelettes, or added to rice wine. Pickling and drying whatever's in season is also part of local life, from *thịt trâu gác bếp* (smoked buffalo jerky) to *thịt ướp chua* (fermented beef or buffalo) and *cá suối ướp chua* (pickled freshwater fish).

Sapa specialities

Much of the remote northwest is relatively inaccessible, but not so Sapa. The region's best known and most tourist-friendly town, Sapa is used by a host of trekking companies as a starting point for multi-day hikes through the region. There's also plenty of great food to sample – we've picked out six of the best local specialities.

CƠM LAM

This sticky rice dish once sustained ethnic minority hunter-gatherers on their long trips through the jungle. After soaking for up to eight hours, the rice is stuffed into tubes of fresh green bamboo with water and ginger, and the whole thing is wrapped in banana leaves and cooked over a fire. It's usually served with grilled meat and sesame seeds.

CỐN SỦI

Sometimes called *phở khan,* the so-called 'dry phở' has its origins in neighbouring China, and is known for its mix of sour, salty, sweet and spicy flavours. Noodles and a gelatinous pork sauce (rather than a broth) are topped with char siu pork, fresh herbs, egg and strips of fried sweet potato, and sprinkled with chilli and peanuts. Some vendors make their dish extra colourful with a mix of purple and orange sweet potato.

LỢN CẮP NÁCH

Named 'armpit pig' for its diminutive size, this indigenous breed of pig is small enough to be carried to the market under one arm. Families usually allow their mini-porkers to roam freely, which adds to their flavour; they're usually roasted and are a staple of wedding feasts.

© marie martin / Getty Images

Left: *Cơm lam*, rice cooked in bamboo
Right: Lunch on the hop in Lao Cai
Below: Flower H'mong traders at Bac Ha market near Sapa

© Gonzalo Azumendi / Getty Images

© Jacob Maentz / Getty Images

STREETSIDE BARBECUE

Every evening, in the Sapa Night Market and along the 'grilling street' of Ham Rong, you'll find rows of stalls selling wooden skewers threaded with pork, fish, chicken wings, chicken feet, mushrooms, tofu, corn, cassava and frog. Once you've made your selection from what's available, the skewers are cooked to order.

THẮNG CỐ

Originally an H'mong dish, this horsemeat soup was a practical meal that made use of animals past working age. It's now a popular dish for domestic Vietnamese visiting Sapa, and is served on the streets and in restaurants. The soup includes horsemeat and organs, plus vegetables, chilli and lemongrass.

XÔI MÀU

Many of the ethnic minority communities of Vietnam's northwest prepare coloured sticky rice, usually as a festival dish, using dyes from local fruits and leaves to provide the culinary kaleidoscope. The hues of the five-colour *xôi ngũ sắc* sticky rice prepared by the Tày people represent the elements of life: yellow for earth, green for plants, red for fire, white for metal and black for water.

The Nung minority group are known for their distinctive seven-colour sticky rice, *xôi bảy màu*. Each of the colours serves as a reminder of the struggles that the Nung peoples have undergone: dark red represents blood spilled, yellow is the colour of heartbreak, bright red symbolises triumph over adversity, and so on.

NORTHEAST VIETNAM

Enclosed by the Hoang Lien Son mountain range to the west, the Chinese border to the north and with its east coast lapped by the waters of the Gulf of Tonkin, Vietnam's cool northeast promises seafood, seasonal produce and a smorgasbord of rice dishes.

NORTHEASTERN CUISINE

Home to 40 ethnic groups, the northeast is known for its stunning rice terraces and waterfalls; its equally easy-on-the-eye coastline encompasses island-dotted Halong Bay, the major tourist drawcard of Quang Ninh province. Unsurprisingly, given the lay of the land, the main culinary highlight here is seafood, from squid and horseshoe crab to mantis shrimp, as well as wetland-dwelling sandworms – all readily available around Halong City.

Aside from fruits of the sea, the speciality of landlocked Bac Giang province is a *cua đá*, a purple land-crab available in the ninth and tenth lunar months, which is often steamed with beer. Lang Son province is the home of *phở chua*, or sour phở, an interesting take on the traditional recipe. More of a warm noodle salad than a soup, it's a mix of noodles, char siu pork, Chinese sausage, fried cakes of sweet potato, offal, cucumber and roasted peanuts, all slathered in a tangy sauce. Another notable Lang Son creation is *khâu nhục*, a stewed pork dish originally from Guangdong in China, and adapted by the Tày and Nung as a feast dish. In Ha Giang and Tuyen Quang provinces, *lợn tên lửa* ('rocket pig') is a local speciality. These small black pigs have bristles that look like rockets launching off their skin.

HÀ GIANG'S POISONOUS PORRIDGE

The residents of this far northern province, up on the border with China, have a saying that goes something like 'if you haven't eaten cháo ấu tẩu*, you haven't been to Ha Giang'. But before you scoff down a bowl of this warm, porky rice porridge on a cold night, consider the main ingredient:* ấu tẩu*, the poisonous monkshood, wolf's bane or aconite plant. The locals eat a lot of it, and* cháo ấu tẩu *vendors will tell you they've soaked and cooked these roots long enough to leech out all the poison. It's said that everyone has a different level of tolerance to the poisons in* ấu tẩu *– but it's perhaps better to be safe than sorry.*

© HuyThoai / Getty Images

Above: Nho Que River Valley, Ha Giang province

© JunPhoto / Shutterstock

© I.S.S Photography / Getty Images

Above: Hanoi's signature *bún chả*
Left: Halong Bay

Halong & Quang Ninh Specialities

BÁNH GẬT GÙ

Similar to *phở cuốn*, this is a rolled-up, steamed rice-flour crepe, served with a dipping sauce and a small bowl of spicy minced pork. The 'nodding cake' name refers to the movement made by the long, springy roll when you pick it up to eat – and perhaps to the nod of satisfaction you'll give once it's in your mouth.

CHẢ MỰC

These little fried patties of pounded squid can be eaten on their own, but are also served with noodles or sticky rice.

CHÁO HÀU

Vietnam's ubiquitous rice porridge, made here with local acorn barnacles.

SÁ SÙNG

Sandworms are best eaten during their late September and early October season; they're served as *canh sá sùng* (sandworm noodle soup), stir-fried or as *chả rươi,* a deep-fried sandworm omelette.

HANOI

Both a province and a city, Vietnam's political and cultural capital celebrated its thousand-year anniversary in 2010. And as long as there have been people living in Hanoi, there have been cooks serving up delicious food to keep the locals warm in winter and cool in summer.

Above: A grand approach to Hanoi's Temple of Literature

© Greg Elms / Lonely Planet

Top: *Bún bò nam bộ*
Bottom: *Bánh cuốn*

© James Pham / Lonely Planet

Hanoi specialities

BÁNH CUỐN

Thin, steamed rice-flour crepes stuffed with minced pork and wood-ear mushrooms, and topped with fried shallots. The *nước chấm* dipping sauce sometimes contains a drop of *cà cuống*, an essence based on water-beetle pheromones.

BÁNH TÔM

Fried sweet potato fritters topped with a small prawn, usually served with lettuce and fresh herbs for wrapping, and a *nước chấm* dipping sauce.

BÚN BÒ NAM BỘ

The name means southern-style beef noodles, but this combination of marinated strips of beef with fresh herbs, cucumber, peanuts, bean sprouts and noodles has become a Hanoi speciality, and is almost impossible to find in the south. It evolved after 1954 when hundreds of southerners migrated north to answer Ho Chi Minh's call to support the Viet Cong.

BÚN CHẢ

For this interactive dish, you add fresh vermicelli noodles, herbs and lettuce to a small bowl of pork patties, sliced grilled pork belly, green papaya and carrot, all swimming in a warm *nước mắm*-based sauce. You can also use a separate small bowl to create different combinations of the ingredients.

BÚN ĐẬU MẮM TÔM

A love-or-hate Hanoi speciality, this is usually a platter of bite-sized items that are dipped in *mắm tôm*, a pungent purple paste made from fermented prawns. The most common dippy-bits are pieces of fried tofu, slices of boiled pork, *chả mực* (squid cake) or *chả cốm* (patties of pork and young green rice), as well as cucumber, fresh herbs and vermicelli noodles. The platter sometimes includes spring rolls and stuffed pork intestine, too.

BÚN RIÊU

A rice-noodle soup with a sweet, sour and savoury tomato broth, usually featuring vermicelli noodles, crab, tofu, shredded *rau muống* (morning glory or water spinach) and squares of congealed pig's blood jelly *(huyết)*. You can also find *bún riêu cá* (with fish) and *bún riêu ốc* (with snails).

BÚN THANG

A chicken and rice-noodle soup, traditionally made on the fourth day of Tết using leftovers from the celebrations. All the ingredients are finely sliced, making it a bit finicky to prepare. The clear broth, made with chicken, pork and dried shrimp, is filled with vermicelli noodles and topped with chicken, *chả lụa* (pork sausage), omelette, shiitake mushrooms and fresh herbs.

CHẢ CÁ LÃ VỌNG

Fish with turmeric, dill and rice noodles, cooked in a tiny pan atop a burner in the middle of your table.

Above: *Bún chả*
Right: Street-food dining in Hanoi's Old Quarter

© Greg Elms / Lonely Planet

PHỞ CUỐN

The literal translation is 'rolled' phở: uncut sheets of phở noodles, wrapped around slices of beef and phở herbs, and dipped into *nước chấm* sauce.

PHỞ

Hanoi-style phở broth should be clear (with a thin layer of oil on top to give it a silky feel) and so full of flavour that nothing needs to be added; it tends to be saltier and more gingery than in other parts of the country. The phở here is usually served with small dishes of bean sprouts, lime wedges and chopped chilli, and the noodles are cut slightly fatter than in the south. Beef phở is the most common in Hanoi, but you can also track down chicken and vegetarian versions.

BÚN CHẢ OBAMA

In May 2016, during filming of his Parts Unknown *foodie travel show, the late chef Anthony Bourdain sat down with Barack Obama to share a simple meal of* bún chả *and beers at Hanoi's Bún chả Hương Liên. The event became an international sensation, propelling this unassuming noodle joint to dizzying heights of fame and making* bún chả *just as famous a Hanoian dish as phở. You don't have to visit Bún chả Hương Liên to eat awesome noodles in Hanoi – but if you do, you'll find the table, chairs and plates used by their famous patrons preserved in a glass cabinet. You'll also find 'combo Obama' on the menu: a serving of* bún chả*, a seafood spring roll and a Hanoi beer, which will set you back the equivalent of around US$3.50.*

Above: Leafy central Haiphong

HAIPHONG

Haiphong is northern Vietnam's second-largest city and one of the country's biggest ports. Seafood is very popular, and the tree-lined boulevards of its appealingly laidback centre host hip cafés where tables spill onto the pavements – perfect for people-watching over a slow-drip coffee *(cà phê phin).*

Haiphong specialities

© 8Creative.vn / Getty Images

Above: Colourful *bánh đa cua*

BÁNH ĐA CUA

A noodle soup with many colours: brownish noodles made from sliced rice crackers, a crab cake, pork meatballs, minced pork wrapped in betel leaves, *rau muống* (morning glory/ water spinach) and tomato.

BÁNH ĐÚC TÀU

A cake of rice- or corn-flour topped with minced pork, ground shrimp, fried onion, sesame seeds, peanuts and fish sauce.

BÁNH MÌ QUE CAY

The local version of bánh mì is a long, thin baguette filled with pâté and chilli sauce. Sometimes called stick bread, though the direct translation is 'spicy baguette'.

BÚN BỀ BỀ

Another tangy dish featuring fresh vermicelli noodles and a tamarind-based broth, *bún bề bề* also features a couple of purplish mantis prawns, pieces of fried tofu, sliced tomato and some greens.

BÚN CÁ CAY

Haiphong's fishy local version of noodle soup features fried fishcakes *(chả cá)* made with mackerel, dill and turmeric, and slices of fried fish. The spicy broth has the tang of tamarind and the funky flavour of fermented bamboo shoots.

NEM CUA BỀ

Square-shaped spring rolls stuffed with a mixture of crab, pork, carrots, mushrooms and glass noodles. They're usually served with fresh noodles and herbs, and a dipping sauce made with locally produced *nước mắm*.

Above: The coastal train between Hue and Hoi An

Right: Hoi An's Cantonese Assembly Hall
Below: Hoi An speciality *cao lầu*

© Flash Parker / Getty Images

CENTRAL VIETNAM

The food of central Vietnam spans a wide spectrum, from the fanciful and elaborate imperial cuisine of Hue to the cheap and cheerful seafood prepared streetside in the coastal areas.

OF KINGS AND CHILLIES

The geographical heart of the nation has a rich history that is reflected in its food, especially so in Hue, imperial capital from 1802 to 1945. A complex and ornate cuisine emerged during the Nguyen Dynasty era: each meal consisted of multiple specialities, and as a result the size of each dish was reduced. Everyday Hue cuisine still reflects this custom in delicious bite-size dishes such as *bánh bèo* and *ram ít* prawn pancakes.

The cuisine of central Vietnam is also known as the country's spiciest. The cooks of Hue are infatuated with the local bird's eye chillies, and the food has a longstanding reputation for being eye-wateringly hot. But these days, local restaurants tend to prepare milder dishes, serving them with a side-bowl of chillies for those who want to ramp up the heat. The most famous of Hue's specialities, *bún bò Huế* is a beef and noodle soup that does pack a punch but looks spicier than it actually is thanks to the inclusion of chilli-red annatto oil.

Down by the sea lie the coastal cities of Danang, Nha Trang, Quy Nhon, Mui Ne and Phan Thiet, where the seafood is plentiful and cheap. All are popular visitor hotspots with a glut of tourist-oriented restaurants serving cold beer and Western-style pizza, pasta and hamburgers alongside 'what tourists think Vietnamese food is'; thankfully, it's easy to sidestep all of this in favour of authentic local cooking.

INTERNATIONAL INFLUENCES

The unique heritage jewel of Hoi An is a foodie hotspot of central Vietnam. This riverside city was a busy international port until the late 18th century, with culinary influences provided by traders and settlers from Europe, China, Japan and India; today, Hoi An's kitchens, street stalls and restaurants source fresh herbs from the organic farms of nearby Tra Que village.

Inland, the central highlands are more famous for tea and coffee than for food. The former French hill station of Dalat is the culinary capital here (and a popular honeymoon destination for Vietnamese couples), with a bustling night-time street food scene, quaint little cafés and higher-end restaurants catering to international visitors.

Opposite page from left to right: *Bún bò Huế, Bún thịt nướng, Cơm hến*

HUE

The chefs of Hue's former imperial court elevated eating to an art form, and a focus on perfect presentation has been retained in family and restaurant kitchens. Hue cuisine is all about tasty small bites, spicy soups and the flavours of the fields, mountains and rivers.

HUE'S IMPERIAL CUISINE

Hue is notable for having two types of cuisine: everyday dishes and the upscale imperial cuisine, developed for the tables of the 13 Nguyen emperors who ruled here between 1802 and 1945. According to legend, the most demanding was Emperor Tu Duc (1848–1883), who expected each meal to include 50 dishes, created by 50 chefs and served by 50 servants. These spectacular feasts included extravagant, intricate dishes, artfully arranged to resemble peacocks, dragons, porcupines and turtles; and as well as being eye-catching, each imperial dish was supposed to have the perfect balance of colour and taste. Today, however, though many restaurants around Hue offer 'imperial cuisine', most of the dishes look a lot better than they taste. What was once food fit for kings is now, sadly, prepared with tourist buses and Instagram in mind. But aside from the fussiness of imperial-style cuisine, Hue does boast a host of more down-to-earth specialities.

Above: Gate over the Imperial Palace moat, Hue

© Oóphoto / Shutterstock

Hue specialities

BÚN BÒ HUẾ

This beef and noodle dish has a sweet, spicy lemongrass-scented broth made with oxtail, beef shank and pork knuckles; annatto provides the distinctive red colour. The noodles are topped with beef slices and ham hocks, and sometimes cubes of pig's blood jelly and crab cakes, and served with a side of fresh herbs, shredded banana bud and bean sprouts. (Pro tip: in Hue, this dish is simply known as *bún bò*; in other parts of the country it's *bún bò Huế*.)

BÚN THỊT NƯỚNG

A bowl of fresh vermicelli noodles over fresh herbs, bean sprouts, pickled veg and lettuce, and topped with lemongrass-marinated barbecued pork, peanuts and fried shallots, perhaps sliced spring rolls as well. The Hue version comes with a warm peanut sauce, used either as a dressing or a dipping sauce.

CHÈ

According to urban legend, there are 36 types of *chè* in Hue; the reality is that there are probably a lot more than that. A popular snack in the evenings, this sweet 'soup' can be served hot or cold, and made with beans, lotus seed, taro, fruit, corn and coconut milk – there's even a savoury version with roast pork *(thịt quay)*.

CƠM HẾN

A bowl of rice topped with tiny river clams, peanuts, sesame seeds, fried pork skin, fresh herbs and fermented shrimp paste, served with a small bowl of spicy clam broth.

NEM LỤI HUẾ

Stalks of lemongrass are used as skewers in this tasty DIY dish. Take a sheet of rice paper, add fresh herbs, cucumber strips, pickles, lettuce and the pork (remove the skewer first), then roll it all up and dip it into the peanut-and-pork dipping sauce.

SNACKING HUE-STYLE

Hue's many specialities include an array of bite-sized morsels, sometimes served by the dozen. Keep your eyes peeled for bánh bèo, *a rice-flour pancake topped with a prawn, powdered dried prawns and a crouton-like piece of fried pork fat;* ram ít, *a tiny prawn encased in crunchy batter, topped with a soft rice pancake and a sprinkle of powdered dried shrimp;* chả tôm, *a prawn cake; and* bánh khoái, *a fried pancake stuffed with pork, prawn and bean sprouts and served with slices of green fig, lettuce, herbs and a tangy dipping sauce.*

DANANG

Above: *Mít trộn* jackfruit salad
Opposite: *Bún mắm nêm* – Danang-style pork and noodles

A dynamic and rapidly growing commercial hub, Danang is surrounded by rivers, mountains and the sea, which deliver wonderful seafood, plentiful fresh produce and a lively street-food scene.

A SEAFOOD CITY

Known as the city of bridges and the gateway to Hoi An, Danang is one of Vietnam's great seafood cities, with crab, lobster, clams, squid, prawns, fish and even jellyfish making regular appearances at local eating joints, which include a host of excellent street-food options.

The city's restaurant scene is becoming more cosmopolitan by the day, and there's a lively café culture too. But the small local places are where you'll find the most authentic dishes, such as *bún chả cá* and *bánh canh* noodle soups, and the local take on fresh spring rolls, *bánh tráng cuốn thịt heo.*

Danang specialities

© Phuong D. Nguyen / Shutterstock

BÁNH CANH

When you order this Danang-style *bánh canh* soup, there are usually three types of noodles to choose from: *bột mì* (made from wheat), *bột gạo* (from rice) or *bột lọc* (from tapioca). You'll also need to select your protein: pork knuckle, fishcake, crab, snakehead fish or shrimp. Locals also order a stick of Chinese-style fried bread *(giò cháo quẩy)* to tear up and dunk into the broth.

BÁNH TRÁNG CUỐN THỊT HEO

An interactive spread of sliced pork, sliced vegetables, herbs and lettuce, which are bundled together into a rice-paper roll, and served with a ginger, lemongrass and chilli dipping sauce.

BÚN CHẢ CÁ

The main difference between the Danang version of this fish and noodle soup and those in other areas is the vegetables used to make the broth: pumpkin, cabbage, pineapple and bamboo shoots. The broth and fishcakes are spooned over vermicelli noodles, topped with chopped green onion and served with a small plate of lettuce, herbs and bean sprouts.

BÚN MẮM NÊM

Shredded lettuce, cucumber and bean sprouts are placed in a bowl, followed by fresh vermicelli noodles and slices of roast pork. Next come a few spoons of oil seasoned with pungent fermented anchovy paste, and a sauce made with pineapple, garlic, lemongrass, chilli and more anchovy paste. The bowl is then topped with peanuts and fried shallots.

MÍT TRỘN

A simple mixed salad of boiled jackfruit, shredded pig skin, shrimp, peanuts, fried onions, fresh herbs and fish sauce.

RAM CUỐN CẢI

Ram is the central Vietnamese name for spring rolls, and *cải* are mustard leaves. In Danang, these small fried pork and shrimp cylinders are served with rice paper, mustard leaves, pickled papaya and fresh herbs. Wrap it all in rice paper for a spring-roll-within-a-spring-roll.

Hoi An

Opposite: Skewers of deliciousness at Hoi An's main market
Below: Handsome Hoi An at dusk

Seaside Hoi An was once a major port, and its tottering old Japanese merchant houses and ancient tea warehouses create a beguiling scene. Food-wise, it's most famous for its noodle soups and a unique Chinese-influenced dumpling with a beautiful name.

© Matthew Micah Wright / Getty Images

Hoi An's cao lầu

Hoi An's most famous speciality comes with an interesting backstory. Chewy and smoky-tasting, true cao lầu *noodles are supposedly made with water from the Champa-era Ba Le well and lye from the ash of Cham Islands trees. This may once have been true, but given the volume of* cao lầu *consumed daily in Hoi An, it's an unlikely prospect today.* Cao lầu *are still made locally, by hand, and the recipe includes well water and a lye solution; whatever their provenance,* cao lầu *are served in a bowl with slices of flavourful roast pork, bean sprouts, fresh herbs, deep-fried noodle squares and a delicious sweetish broth.*

Hoi An specialities

© James Pham

Though Hoi An's upscale restaurants cook up a host of tourist-friendly dishes that are designed to cater to the tastes of the town's many international visitors, the list of local specialities is quite short. Nonetheless, there are several standouts that are well worth a try. Street food and inexpensive eats at the main market offer some great alternatives to a fine-dining restaurant experience.

BÁNH BAO VẠC

A very Chinese-style dish that's now one of the must-try local specialities, 'white rose dumplings' are the creation of a local family who are still said to be the sole owners of the original recipe. Scrunched up to look like a rose, the delicate rice-flour dumplings are filled with minced prawns and topped with crispy-fried garlic and *nước mắm.*

BÁNH MÌ HOI AN

Hoi An is well known for its superlative baguette sandwiches – Anthony Bourdain's *Parts Unknown* coverage made one local vendor, Bánh Mì Phượng, an international superstar and a must-try street-food stop. But there are other bánh mì places that are just as good – or even better.

CƠM GÀ

Considering Hoi An's history as a trading port, the proximity of Hainan (only 300km/186 miles away) and the Vietnamese love of adopting standout foods from their neighbours, it's no surprise that 'chicken rice' is a popular dish here. The local version comprises a plate of soft fluffy rice topped with shredded chicken, sliced green papaya and fresh herbs. A small bowl of chicken broth is usually served as a side.

HOÀNH THÁNH CHIÊN

Kind of like a mini pizza, this is a fried wonton topped with a Chinese-ish sweet-and-sour sauce.

MÌ QUẢNG

These Quang-style noodles comprise a rustic bowl of chewy noodles (sometimes coloured yellow with turmeric) mixed with slices of roast pork, shrimp, quail's eggs, fresh herbs, crushed peanuts and shards of toasted rice crackers, all doused in a sweet-and-savoury broth. One story says the noodles hark back to the 14th century, which may make this a much more authentic local dish than *cao lầu.*

Opposite: Spicy *bánh canh chả cá*

QUY NHON

About halfway between Danang and Nha Trang, the quiet little seaside town of Quy Nhon in Binh Dinh province offers stellar street food, and is also a great place to indulge in a seafood session.

A WALK DOWN 'EATING STREET'

Despite its terrific beaches, Quy Nhon hasn't been on the tourist radar for very long, though a crop of new cafés and bars has injected a dose of cosmopolitan cool. Most international visitors head directly to one of the town's fancy self-contained resorts and rarely venture out, missing out on the town's culinary highlight: street food. Head to Quy Nhon's 'eating street', Ngo Van So, to sample the local versions of *bánh xèo* and *bánh canh cá*. Don't miss the local seafood, either: scallops, clams, oysters, prawns, squid, crab and fish are all excellent.

Quy Nhon specialities

BÁNH CANH CHẢ CÁ

A delicious peppery soup with slices of fishcake and thick, chewy tapioca noodles.

BÁNH MÌ RAGU

Adapted from the French *ragout*, this hearty beef, carrot and potato stew is served with a baguette, to be torn into chunks and dipped into the sauce.

BÁNH XÈO

Quy Nhon's sizzling savoury pancakes are smaller than the southern Vietnamese original; the pancake itself chewier and beige rather than bright yellow. Wrap them up with rice paper, cucumber slices, bean sprouts and fresh herbs, and dip in the warm sesame sauce.

BÚN RẠM

A popular breakfast dish featuring vermicelli noodles, fresh herbs, lettuce and minced crab in a spicy broth.

BÚN TÔM

Often available at places that serve *bún rạm*, this version has prawns rather than crab. The broth can be rather bland, which can be remedied with a dash of fermented fish paste.

PHU YEN SPECIALITIES

South of Quy Nhon, the coastal towns of Phu Yen province promise more delicious seafood. Don't miss the bánh canh hẹ, *a chive-heavy fishcake soup with tapioca noodles. You might also want to try a more challenging local dish:* mắt cán gừ, *or tuna eyeballs. Not a traditional Vietnamese delicacy,* mắt cán gừ *was created by local cooks who read about the Korean and Japanese tradition of eating tuna eyeballs (a part of the fish usually discarded in Vietnam) and wanted to try it for themselves. Tuna eyeballs are now served several ways in Phu Yen, perhaps deep-fried or forming the centrepiece of a flavourful soup that's often served in a bowl atop a flaming table-top spirit cooker – a pretty sight at night.*

NHA TRANG

Known for its classic combination of sun, sand and seafood, party-hard Nha Trang draws in hordes of visitors. Skip the tourist-trap restaurants and follow the locals to the seafood joints along the Cai River waterfront or north of Tran Phu bridge.

Nha Trang specialities

BÁNH CĂN NHA TRANG

Taking advantage of the bounty of the sea, the Nha Trang version of these mini rice-flour pancakes includes prawn and squid. As well as *nước chấm* dipping sauce, some outlets also serve *bánh căn* with a small bowl of pork-meatball soup.

BÁNH ƯỚT

These 'wet cakes' are large steamed rice crepes, served flat or rolled, dusted with chopped green onion and fried shallots, with a *nước chấm* dipping sauce and slices of *chả lụa* (pork sausage). *Bánh ướt* places usually serve *bánh hỏi* (lattice noodles) and *bánh bèo* (small rice-flour pancakes) too, and sometimes all three are combined in one serving.

BÁNH XÈO MỰC

The Nha Trang version of this sizzling savoury pancake is smaller than the original southern Vietnamese dish, and not all outlets colour the pancake yellow with turmeric. Some places stuff the pancake with squid, pork and bean sprouts; at others there'll be some prawns in there as well; all serve them with fresh herbs and a dipping sauce.

BÚN CHẢ CÁ

A noodle soup with slices of fishcake, tuna and tomato, with a side of fresh herbs and shredded lettuce or cabbage.

BÚN SỨA

Very similar to *bún chả cá*, but with slices of jellyfish and fishcake. It's considered a cooling dish, perfect for a hot summer's day.

NEM NƯỚNG NHA TRANG

A colourful platter of ingredients – *nem* (fried rice-paper rolls), cucumber, lettuce, fresh herbs, noodles – to be wrapped in rice paper. What sets the Nha Trang version apart from other regional variations is the dipping sauce, a bright-orange mixture of minced pork and annatto oil.

© Elena Aleksandrovna Ermakova / Getty Images

Above: *Bánh xèo*
Below: Nha Trang's Po Nagar Cham towers

© Diego Fiore / Getty Images

A BLAST FROM THE PAST

Just west of Nha Trang, with a collection of tiled and palm-thatched huts arranged around a lotus pond, Nha Trang Xưa ('ancient Nha Trang') is a classic Vietnamese restaurant. Everything here is a nostalgic nod to an idealised pastoral past, from the kitchen garden to the handwritten menu and, of course, the food: perhaps fish barbecued in bamboo or a delicious clay-pot concoction. Whatever you order, dining here offers an atmospheric step back in time.

MUI NE & PHAN THIET

With a string of resorts that have pretty much eclipsed the original fishing village, Mui Ne's food scene is targeted squarely at domestic and international tourists. For more authentic dining, head to nearby Phan Thiet for seafood, local staples – and maybe even some lizard.

Opposite: Mui Ne's busy fishing scene
Below: Sand dunes at Mui Ne

© Det-anan / Shutterstock

NƯỚC MẮM CENTRAL

The bustling port of Phan Thiet has long been known for its *nước mắm* (fish sauce), producing millions of litres of this pungent condiment each year. The backbone of Vietnamese cooking, *nước mắm* is often diluted down with water, lime juice and sugar to become the *nước chấm* dipping sauce that's so ubiquitous on Vietnamese tables; unsurprisingly, it's an essential element of many Phan Thiet specialities.

Phan Thiet specialities

BÁNH CĂN PHAN THIẾT

A 'sandwich' of two small, grilled rice-flour pancakes filled with green onion and chives, served with slivered green mango and a bowl of soup. Mix all the ingredients together to taste.

BÁNH QUAI VẠC

These translucent tapioca dumplings (sometimes called *bột lọc*) are stuffed with shrimp and served with *nước mắm*.

CHẢ CUỐN PHAN THIẾT

Another roll-your-own dish consisting of plates of peppery pork sausage, fermented pork, roast pork, lemongrass pork sausage, a boiled egg, green mango strips, cucumber, spring rolls, fresh herbs and a tangy dipping sauce.

DÔNG LIZARD

The farmed variety of the local *dông* lizard is considered an environmentally friendly and sustainable food source hereabouts. The lizards can be barbecued, made into spring rolls or incorporated into a salad or rice porridge.

GỎI CÁ MAI

Raw fish, usually whitebait, marinated ceviche-style in lime juice, then coated with roasted rice flour and mixed with slices of onion and crushed peanuts, and served alongside fresh herbs, slices of cucumber, green banana, star fruit, rice paper and a dipping sauce – you create your own fresh spring roll.

RĂNG MỰC NƯỚNG

The direct translation of the name is 'grilled octopus teeth', but these barbecued squid skewers are actually made with the mouth or beak of the octopus, which is usually discarded; they taste a little like chewy chicken cartilage.

© HeadHog / Shutterstock

DALAT AND THE CENTRAL HIGHLANDS

With coffee plantations, pine-studded mountains and peaceful villages home to the Jarai, M'nong, Ede and Bannar peoples, Vietnam's beautiful but sparsely populated central highlands (Tây Nguyên) are supremely scenic. Outside of the main centre, Dalat, the cuisine is mostly simple fare: roast chicken *(gà nướng)* or pork *(heo rẫy nướng)*, and bamboo rice *(cơm lam)*.

DALAT

Established by the French as a hill station in 1912 in a bid to escape the heat of the steamy lowlands, Dalat doesn't have a lengthy culinary tradition. Migrants from other parts of Vietnam have added local tweaks to staples such as phở and turmeric-yellow *mì Quảng* noodles, but the cooking here is all about taking advantage of the cool climate and abundant local produce to create food that warms the stomach and the soul.

Dalat is known for the fresh, temperate-climate vegetables grown on the farms surrounding the town; visiting Vietnamese head to the central market to load up with cabbages, carrots, onions and potatoes, which are then spirited back to their hometowns. Artichokes are another speciality here, but bear in mind that as artichoke soup is considered medicinal, it's not expected to taste good – and it doesn't. It's better to stick to the sweet and slightly nutty artichoke tea.

Dalat's market also has picture-perfect stalls laden with the hydrangeas, fuchsias and orchids grown in nearby flower farms, and vendors selling candied locally grown strawberries, mulberries and other fruit. At night, don't miss the pop-up street food stalls that set up around the market.

Below from top to bottom: *Nem nướng*; Dalat street food stall

Dalat specialities

BÁNH CĂN ĐÀ LẠT

A mini rice-flour pancake topped with a quail egg, served with pork meatballs and a sweet fish-sauce-based dipping sauce.

BÁNH ƯỚT LÒNG GÀ ĐÀ LẠT

A little like a warm salad, with wide noodles topped by chicken, offal, fresh herbs, onion and fried shallots. It's possible to order it with no offal: ask for 'không lòng'.

BÁNH MÌ XÍU MẠI ĐÀ LẠT

Something like a deconstructed meatball sub, this is a small bowl of meatballs swimming in pork broth, served with a mini bánh mì that you dip into the soup.

BÚN THỐ ĐÀ LẠT

A warming soup of vermicelli noodles, fishcakes, prawns and pork swimming in a broth made with pork bones and coconut water. Add a squeeze of lime and fresh herbs according to your preference.

© marie martin / Getty Images

© Joel Whalton / Shutterstock

BÁNH TRÁNG ĐÀ LẠT

Made every evening near the market, the so-called Dalat pizza is a rice-paper base slathered with a mixture of egg, dried baby shrimp, chopped green onions and a sweet and spicy sauce, which is barbecued on a charcoal brazier then rolled up.

NEM NƯỚNG

A roll-your-own experience that involves rice paper, barbecued *nem* (fermented pork), fresh herbs, fried rice-paper rolls and pickled vegetables.

TÂY NGUYÊN CUISINE

The provinces of the central highlands have several notable specialities. Pleiku in Gia Lai is known for its phở khô Gia Lai *(Gia Lai-style dry phở), a multi-bowl affair with one dish containing broth, another noodles, another for bean sprouts, a small plate for fresh herbs, chilli and lime wedges and at least one tiny dish to hold a dipping sauce.* Bún riêu *(crab and noodle soup) is popular in Pleiku and Buon Me Thuot, while* bún đỏ Đắk Lắk *is the most famous dish of Dak Lak province. It's a tasty noodle soup with crab cake, pork rind, boiled eggs and some greens, served with a side of bean sprouts and a lime wedge.*

Opposite: Beachside eating in Phu Quoc
Below: Con Dao island

© studioloco / Shutterstock

SOUTHERN VIETNAM

Hot, tropical southern Vietnam promises a vibrant food scene in the commercial hub of Ho Chi Minh City, while the Mekong Delta, known as the nation's rice bowl, offers an abundance of fresh produce.

SOUTHERN CUISINE

Vietnam's laid-back southerners are obsessed with eating, drinking and snacking, and the food here is characterised by herb-heavy shared meals, accompanied by lots of noisy toasting. The tropical climate delivers an abundance of locally grown fruits and vegetables, as well as bountiful fish and seafood from inland waterways and the ocean – southern cooks have a diverse range of ingredients to work with.

Southern cuisine has also been influenced by the area's history. From the 1st to the 6th centuries CE, the Mekong Delta was the centre of the Indianised Cambodian kingdom of Funan, a collection of city-states that had trading links with China, Indonesia, Persia and even parts of the Mediterranean. Chinese immigration to southern Vietnam began in the first century, and

several waves of migration followed; today, the Mekong Delta is home to significant populations of ethnic Chinese and Khmer, as well as a smaller Cham community.

How this history influences modern southern Vietnamese cooking is a matter of speculation. Though more common as a home-cooked dish than something on offer at street-food stalls or restaurants, the south's *cà ri gà* (chicken curry) could have evolved from Funan's Indian influence, or from the Indian cooks brought here by the French during their era of rule. Equally, *cà ri gà* is a coconut and lemongrass curry – coconut milk is not that common in Vietnamese cooking, but widely used in Cambodia and Thailand. And to add a final level of confusion, *cà ri gà* is usually served with a baguette, which is obviously a French influence. But for most southern Vietnamese cooks, the origins of their recipes aren't terribly important; instead, the focus is on creating the most flavourful food from fresh local ingredients.

CULINARY HOTSPOTS

Hanoi may consider itself more cultured, but Ho Chi Minh City is Vietnam's culinary capital, with delicious southern specialities complemented by Indian, Japanese, Korean, Thai, Italian and East-West fusion restaurants, as well as plenty of places serving French cuisine. Down on the coast, Vũng Tàu is a popular getaway for the Saigonese, and has many delicious local and international eateries, while the offshore islands of Con Dao and Phu Quoc are gorgeous visitor honeypots with a range of mid-range and upscale places that make the most of locally caught seafood.

HO CHI MINH CITY

Below left: Ho Chi Minh City *chè* stall
Below right: Head to District 1 for a Ho Chi Minh City dim sum fix

© Lonely Planet

© Godong/robertharding / Getty Images

High-octane Ho Chi Minh City is Vietnam at its most dizzying, a commercial and cultural whirl that offers both the classiest of restaurants and the tastiest of street food.

VIETNAM'S CULINARY CAPITAL

Formerly Saigon (and still widely referred to as such), Ho Chi Minh City is in the grip of a food and craft beer renaissance, with new international and fusion outlets popping up every second week. A beer, barbecue and burger craze has swept through the city in recent years, followed closely by a tapas revolution. Japanese and Korean food has been plentiful for some time, especially among the city's large expat community. But despite the onslaught of the new, street-food stalls, family restaurants and little *quán ăn* serving strictly Vietnamese food remain the choice of the masses.

Ho Chi Minh City specialities

BÁNH BAO
A local version of China's *baozi*, these fluffy steamed buns are common street-food snacks, stuffed with minced pork, mushroom and quail's eggs. Some versions also have salted eggs inside; dim sum places and Chinatown restaurants have other fillings, too.

BÒ BÍT TẾT
A breakfast dish of sizzling beefsteak served on a hot, cow-shaped griddle that continues to cook the steak, eggs and pâté after it's brought to the table. Usually served with lettuce, tomato slices and a baguette.

BÒ LÁ LỐT
Beef sautéed with lemongrass, wrapped in betel leaves into a thin sausage-shape and then grilled over charcoal to release the bitter, peppery flavour of the leaves.

BÒ LÚC LẮC
Seared cubes of marinated steak 'shaken' in a pan with garlic and onion, served on a bed of lettuce or watercress. If served sizzling, the dish usually includes sweet peppers and a small side of French fries.

BỘT CHIÊN
This local take on China's carrot or radish cakes is a square rice-flour cake, topped with a fried egg and shredded green papaya and slathered with a tangy, sweet soy sauce.

BÚN THỊT NƯỚNG
Soft, fresh vermicelli noodles, piquant marinated barbecued pork, lettuce, fresh herbs and *nước chấm*; the components are served in separate sections so that diners can mix, fold and season their *bún thịt nướng* to taste.

CÀ RI GÀ
A sweet yellow curry of lemongrass, ginger, chicken pieces, sweet potato, taro and carrots. It's usually not spicy, and is served with rice or a toasted baguette.

CANH CHUA CÁ
Served at the end of a meal, this sour fish soup is an everyday favourite. It's sweetened with chunks of pineapple and tomato, the sour flavour comes from tamarind, and it also includes sliced okra, elephant-ear stem and bean sprouts.

CLAY-POT COOKING
Found throughout southern Vietnam, earthenware clay pots are used to cook a host of intensely flavoured regional dishes, which usually have a thick base incorporating fish sauce and caramelised sugar. Some of the best clay-pot classics are built around fish (cá kho tộ) *and prawns* (tôm kho tộ)*; the Tết favourite* thịt kho tàu *(pork and duck eggs braised in coconut water) is especially delicious.*

© James Pham / Lonely Planet

Above: Vietnam's culinary capital promises a buzzing street-food scene

© marie martin / Getty Images

Above: *Hủ tiếu* is a must-try Ho Chi Minh City speciality

CƠM TẤM

Originally a peasant dish that utilised the cheapest type of rice (grains broken during harvesting) as a base for various toppings, *cơm tấm* has evolved into a cheap and cheerful meal for all. Topping ingredients are displayed in glass cases, and you order from what's available; classic choices include *sườn* (barbecued pork chop) and slices of *chả trứng* (a pork and glass-noodle quiche).

GỎI CUỐN

Directly translated as 'rolled salad', but known to English-speakers as a summer roll or rice-paper roll, *gỏi cuốn* are prawn, pork, fresh vermicelli noodles, bean sprouts and herbs rolled in softened rice paper. Served with a hoisin or *nước chấm* dipping sauce.

HỦ TIẾU

Brought to Vietnam some 300 years ago by migrants from China's Guangdong province, *hủ tiếu* is now a popular Saigonese speciality, with glass noodles, prawns, pork and quail's eggs in a pork-based broth, served with a little plate of bean sprouts, chives, edible chrysanthemum, lettuce, lime and chilli. *Hủ tiếu* can be served 'wet' *(nước)* as a soup, or 'dry' *(khô)* with a small bowl of broth on the side.

PHỞ

Southern-style phở is served with an abundance of fresh herbs (Thai basil, sawtooth coriander, Vietnamese balm and rice-paddy herb), bean sprouts and condiments. Each diner prepares their dish according to their preferences. Some like it hot (adding extra chilli), some like it sweeter (via a squirt of hoisin sauce) and some like different cuts of meat. The most basic versions are beef, chicken and vegetarian. Southern phở noodles are cut thinner than the northern version.

RAU LUỘC KHO QUẸT

A dish that harks back to the lean years, when food had to be stretched as much as possible. Plain vegetables – okra, bok choi, carrot and cucumber – are served with an intensely flavoured dipping sauce made from pork fat, dried shrimp, fish sauce, pepper and sugar.

CHINESE SPECIALITIES

Ho Chi Minh City's Chinatown is not a compact and well-defined area; the city's Chinese-Vietnamese population – and their food stalls and restaurants – are spread throughout Districts 9, 10 and, especially, District 5 (Cholon), with its temples and Chinese-style architecture. Here and all around the city you'll find restaurants and street stalls selling delicious Chinese cuisine. Staples include the following:

- **Chinese-style barbecue** *Rows of barbecued ducks and baby pigs hanging in a window signify that you've found a barbecue shop. You can buy the whole animal, a few slices, or a bánh mì filled with your choice of barbecued meat.*

- **Dim sum** *Ho Chi Minh City's dim sum restaurants serve all of the usual bite-sized treats. Some places have the rolling carts; others take orders à-la-carte.*

- **Gà hầm thuốc bắc** *Made with black-boned silkie chickens, considered more nutritious than regular birds, the medicinal value of this herbal soup is further boosted by goji berries, ginger, jujube fruits, lotus seeds and mushrooms. There's often a whole chicken hiding in the broth, head and all.*

- **Mì hoành thánh** *Pork-and-prawn wontons with yellow noodles in a pork broth.*

- **Mì vịt tiềm** *The Chinese flavours of five-spice lend a subtle fragrance to this duck and yellow-noodle soup.*

- **Súp cua** *A gelatinous and peppery soup with crab, mushroom and egg, which can also include corn* (bắp) *or asparagus* (măng tây).

VUNG TAU

The seaside resort of Vung Tau is an easy day-trip from Ho Chi Minh City, but one day is not enough to eat your way through the local specialities, many featuring fresh-caught seafood.

VUNG TAU

Vung Tau is a laidback place. The streets are wide, the traffic is slow and, unlike bigger, more tourist-oriented towns, the smaller eating places close between meals. Finding a local-style late breakfast or lunch here can prove tricky, so it's best to follow the local example and schedule your day around food; the same applies on Con Dao island.

Vung Tau occupies a strange space in Vietnam's tourist landscape. It's not a popular destination for international visitors, who bypass the city altogether en route to the luxurious all-inclusive resorts strung out between Vung Tau and Ho Tram. But it is a popular vacation spot for domestic tourists, and also has a reasonable expat population, mostly made up of foreign specialists who work on the offshore oil rigs. Consequently, the food scene is a strange hodgepodge of cafés, local food joints (including some huge, shed-like seafood places just out of town) and Western-style restaurants.

Vung Tau is most famous for its *bánh khọt*, the baby cousin of *bánh xeo* (savoury sizzling pancakes), and every visit to this seaside city should include at least one round of its popular breakfast dish.

Left: Loaded *bánh khọt* rice-flour pancakes on the grill

Vung Tau specialities

BÁNH KHỌT

A smaller, sweeter cousin of *bánh xeo* (sizzling pancakes), *bánh khọt* are a bite-sized coconut- and rice-flour version, topped with a prawn, green onion and dried prawn powder. Roll them with herbs in a lettuce or mustard leaf, then dunk the whole thing in the dipping sauce.

BÁNH TIÊU ĐẬU XANH ĐỒ CHIẾU

A light wheat-dough pocket stuffed with a sweet green-bean paste, sprinkled with sesame seeds and fried until golden.

BÁNH ƯỚT DĨA CHỒNG ĐĨA

Translating literally as 'stacked plate wet cake', this dish starts with a steamed rice-flour crepe (the 'wet cake'), served on its own plate. Next, order a plate of barbecued pork or chicken, and another of pickled greens or shredded green mango, then assemble your preferred stuffings and roll up the crepe. Keep ordering and watch the plates pile up.

GỎI CÁ MAI

Almost identical to the Phan Thiet version, this is raw whitebait soaked in lime juice, with onion and crushed peanuts. Pick and choose from the platter served alongside to create your own fish, herb and salad rice-paper wrap.

CON DAO ISLAND

Way out in the South China Sea some 200km (124 miles) south of Vung Tau, and connected by boats and planes from the mainland, this sleepy former prison island is a great place to unwind, with accommodation in all budgets and some excellent local seafood – the must-try specialities are cua mặt trăng *(moon crab),* tôm hùm đỏ *(red lobster) and* cá mú đỏ *(red grouper). There's also* gỏi cá mập*, a local take on the southern Vietnamese raw fish salad, made with slices of baby shark and served with a hot dipping sauce. Con Dao's* bún riêu cua *(rice-paddy crab and noodle soup) is a tasty cheap eat, while the more adventurous might like to sample* mắm nhum*, a fermented dipping sauce made with* nhum *(sea urchin).*

MEKONG DELTA

Thanks to its agricultural economy, the Mekong Delta has an abundance of fresh fruit, vegetables, coconuts and rice, as well as fish, crab and other edibles from the area's brackish wetlands. People tend to eat very simply here, making use of the plentiful and fresh local produce.

WHERE WATER IS LIFE

The Mekong Delta used to be known for its slow pace of life and reliance on the waterways for food and transport. New highways have changed things somewhat – these days, produce is more likely to be loaded onto a truck than a barge. But the water is still vitally important to everyday life. Rice paddies do double-duty as ponds for prawns, fish and eels, and flowering water plants are also a source of food. The beautiful yellow *bông điên điển* (sesbania) flowers, which bloom during the Mekong Delta's flood season (July to November), are used in hot-pots and salads.

As to the local cuisine, while phở might be Vietnam's national dish, the noodle soup of choice here is *hủ tiếu*, evolved from a recipe brought by Chinese migrants hundreds of years ago and packed full of pork, shrimp and fresh vegetables and herbs. A sunrise breakfast of *hủ tiếu* at a floating market on the Mekong is a memorable experience.

Below: Duck herding on a Mekong Delta waterway

Mekong Delta specialities

© Albert Engeln / Getty Images

Above: Table-ready elephant-ear fish

BÁNH XÈO

The bright yellow Mekong Delta *bánh xèo* pancakes are huge, stuffed with pork, shrimp and bean sprouts, served with a platter of fresh herbs and with lettuce and mustard leaves to use as wrappers.

BÚN NƯỚC LÈO

A speciality of Mekong towns Soc Trang and Tra Vinh, this coconut-water broth is flavoured with galangal, lemongrass and a fermented paste *(mắm cá sặc)* made from the elephant-ear fish; the cook adds locally made vermicelli noodles, a few shrimp and slices of fish and pork, and it's usually served with a side of fresh herbs, sliced banana buds and bean sprouts.

CÁ TAI TƯỢNG CHIÊN XÙ

Once a feast dish, fried elephant-ear fish has become a tourist crowd-pleaser. After being fried whole, this large fish is presented upright on a stand. Using chopsticks, you break off a morsel of fish and use it as the base for a rice-paper roll, adding fresh herbs and vegetables. The dipping sauce usually contains fish sauce, tamarind, lemongrass, garlic and chilli. Wait staff will offer to prepare the rolls for you in tourist-friendly places.

CHUỘT ĐỒNG

April to August, the third rice harvest, is peak season for edible field rats in the Mekong Delta – as the *chuột đồng* have grown nice and plump

© SamuelBrownNG / Getty Images

Above: *Hủ tiếu*
Right: Supersized Mekong Delta *bánh xèo*

from extended feasting on the remaining rice. *Chuột đồng* can be grilled with lemongrass and chilli, stewed in coconut water or cooked into a coconut-milk curry.

GÀ KHO SẢ ỚT

A simple dish of chicken pieces, marinated in lemongrass and chilli and then braised.

GÀ NƯỚNG BÙN

This 'mud-roasted chicken' was originally a staple dish for farmers, prepared and eaten in the fields. A whole chicken is wrapped in lotus leaves (or more usually foil these days), and then a layer of mud from the rice paddy. The giant ball is covered in straw, which is set alight and left to burn for an hour or so until the meat is cooked.

HỦ TIẾU

Of the two types of *hủ tiếu* noodle soup made in the Mekong, the version from Mỹ Tho is perhaps the best known, notable for its use of dried shrimp in the broth (which gives it a slightly saltier flavour), its clearer and chewier noodles and the lack of prawns in the soup. You'd be hard-pressed to tell

© vinhdav / Getty Images

© Pinnee / Getty Images

Above: *Nem nướng* pork skewers

the difference between this and the Sa Đéc-style *hủ tiếu*, though it does have long, slightly square-shaped noodles. Both contain slices of pork, offal and quail's eggs, and are served with fresh herbs and bean sprouts.

MẮM DISHES

In the Mekong Delta, this strong-smelling fermented fish or shrimp paste is used as a base for a shared hot-pot, *mắm lẩu*, or for the equally pungent *bún mắm*, rice-noodle soup with shrimp, fish, squid or roasted pork. In the flood season, both dishes usually feature the edible flowers of the *bông điên điển* (sesbania) plant.

NEM NƯỚNG

The Mekong Delta version of these classic pork skewers are larger than in some other places. Once grilled, they're the backbone of a roll-your-own rice-paper roll experience, with fresh herbs, pickled vegetables and a dipping sauce.

PHU QUOC

A lush tropical island surrounded by teaming oceans – what better place to eat seafood? Phu Quoc's specialities include *ghẹ Hàm Ninh* (flower crab from Ham Ninh village), *nhum biển* (sea urchin), *mực* (squid) and *tôm mũ ni* (slipper lobster).

ISLAND CUISINE

Fringed with white-sand beaches and with large tracts still cloaked in dense tropical jungle, Phu Quoc has rapidly morphed from a sleepy island backwater known for its native web-footed dogs, fish-sauce factories and pepper plantations to a must-visit beach escape for Western expats and sun-seeking tourists. As tourism has exploded, so has the resident population and the tourist infrastructure: today, the dining options range from beach bars and quaint cafés to lavish resorts with high-end restaurants.

The night market in the main town, Duong Dong, does a roaring trade in grilled-before-your-eyes seafood such as surf-fresh *cobia* fish (there are vegetarian options too), and also has an array of mid-range Western eateries, from burger bars to German bakeries. Look out, too, for cottage-industry products made on local farms, such as honey or tea infused with local black peppercorns.

Phu Quoc specialities

BÁNH CANH CHẢ CÁ

Tapioca-noodle soup with a chewy mackerel fishcake, served with a spicy dipping sauce and a tiny plate of fresh herbs and vegetables.

BÚN KÈN

This noodle soup reflects Phu Quoc's close proximity to Cambodia. Vermicelli noodles are topped with shredded green papaya, bean sprouts, fresh herbs and minced fish, plus a few ladles of broth made with fish, coconut milk, curry spices and five-spice. Add fresh chilli to taste.

CANH NẤM TRÀM HẢI SẢN

Unusual soup combining slightly bitter *tràm* mushrooms (which grow under Phu Quoc's melaleuca trees during the rainy season) with squid, prawns, minced pork and local black pepper.

GÀ HẤP TIÊU XANH PHÚ QUỐC

Steamed chicken with spicy Phu Quoc green peppercorns.

GỎI CÁ TRÍCH

Raw herring slices, marinated in lime juice and mixed with finely sliced chilli, onions, mint and coconut, and served with rice paper, cucumber slices and fresh herbs to make fish rolls.

MỰC TRỨNG

A finger-sized squid that's caught when full of its eggs. Best fried with Phu Quoc's famous fish sauce, or barbecued with chilli and lemongrass paste.

© Jimmy Tran / Shutterstock

Above: Phu Quoc island promises sun, sand and seafood

VIETNAMESE PHRASES

Though Vietnamese is a tricky language to master, the following phrases will help you navigate a foodie exploration of the country.

LEARNING SOME OF THE LINGO

The US government's Foreign Service Institute gives Vietnamese a difficulty rating of four (in a scale of one to five) in terms of how easily English-speakers can learn the language, ranking it up there with the equally tricky Russian, Thai and Finnish. It's estimated that a learner will need 1100 hours to overcome the significant linguistic and/or cultural differences between Vietnamese and English in order to gain a working knowledge of Vietnamese. While that's well beyond the scope of most travellers, knowing a little bit of Vietnamese (especially how to recognise and pronounce words) will greatly enhance your eating adventures – you'll be able to read basic words on signs and menus, and have some amount of interaction with people at markets, restaurants and food stalls.

The good news is that Vietnamese is one of only a handful of Southeast Asian languages to use a Roman-based script, created by 17th-century Catholic missionaries such as Alexandre de Rhodes. Before that, Vietnamese used a writing system based on Chinese characters, and even today, some estimates suggest that 70% or more of the Vietnamese lexicon is Chinese in origin. There are also many linguistic nods to the French era, mostly confined to the names of food items, from *cà rem* (ice-cream, from the French *crème*) to *gato* (cake, derived from *gateau*) and *bít tết* (beef steak, from *bifteck*).

THE BASICS OF VIETNAMESE

The Vietnamese language has no genders, no plurals and no verb conjugations. Tenses are simple, the grammar is relatively straightforward, and words are pronounced exactly as they appear. While the country's northern, central and southern regions have distinct accents and a few area-specific words, it's essentially the same basic Vietnamese spoken throughout the country.

Another plus is that all Vietnamese words are monosyllabic, with some words combined to make compound words. Vietnamese also uses classifiers, words added in front of nouns to show what group they belong to. For instance, *máy* means machine, *lạnh* means cold – so for air-conditioner, the Vietnamese say *máy lạnh*; for aeroplane, it's *máy bay* (where 'bay' means 'fly'), and so on. This is pretty useful when it comes to food: *thịt* is the classifier for types of meat – so beef is *thịt bò* (literally 'meat cow'), and pork is *thịt heo* ('meat pig'). *Nước* is the classifier for liquids, so *nước cam* is orange juice, *nước suối* mineral water.

The main challenge of Vietnamese for most learners, however, are the tones. Indicated in written words by accents above or below the vowel, Vietnamese has six distinctive tones, some of which were described by none other than Alexandre de Rhodes as 'acute-angry', 'chesty-heavy' and 'grave-lowering'. One single word can mean six different things depending upon tone used, so it's no surprise that visitors can easily get things wrong.

Because no written phonemic guide is ideal for tonal pronunciation, we recommend that you try out some of the phrases on the following pages with a Vietnamese speaker, perhaps someone at your hotel. It's also good to note that the most Vietnamese have had some exposure to English in public school, although more in terms of grammar and reading than listening and speaking.

LOOK OUT FOR ...

- *The letters f, j, w and z are not part of the Vietnamese alphabet, but are sometimes used in informal writing such as text messages*

- *'D' and 'gi' are pronounced like the English 'z' in the north, and like a 'y' in the south*

- *'Đ' and 'đ' (with a stroke) are pronounced like the English 'd'*

What looks like a hat above certain vowels (as in chấm*, meaning dip), like a rice bowl (as per* mắm*, the second part of the Vietnamese word for fish sauce), or like a hook (as in* phở*) aren't accents that change the tone of the word; instead, these marks indicate a different sound for the letter below.*

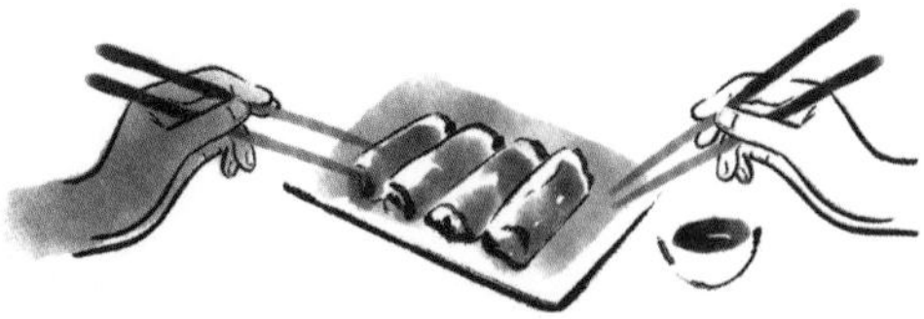

USEFUL DINING OUT PHRASES

Some basic phrases are listed below; where's there's regional variation, we've used (N) to indicate northern Vietnam, and (S) for the south.

Basics

Hello	Xin chào	*sin jòw*
Goodbye	Tạm biệt	*daạm bee·ụht*
Yes	Vâng (N)	*vuhng*
	Dạ (S)	*yạ*
No	Không	*kawm*
Please	Làm ơn	*Laàm ern*
Thank you	Cám ơn	*ğaám ern*
You're welcome	Không có chi	*kawm ğó jee*
Excuse me/sorry	Xin lỗi	*sin lõy*
Breakfast	ăn sáng	*uhn saáng*
Lunch	ăn trưa	*uhn chuhr·uh*
Dinner	ăn tối	*uhn dóy*
Snack	ăn nhẹ	*uhn nyạ*
I'd like ...	Tôi muốn ...	*doy moo·úhn ...*
I'm starving!	Tôi đói dã man!	*doy đóy zaã maan*
Do you speak English?	Bạn có nói được tiếng Anh không?	*baạn ğó nóy đuhr·ẹrk díng aang kawm*
I (don't) understand	Tôi (không) hiểu	*doy (kawm) heẻ·oo*

Cooking methods

Grill	nướng	*nuhr·érng*
Boil	luộc	*loo·ụhrk*
Steam	hấp	*huhrp*
Fry	chiên/rán	*jee·uhn/raáng*
Stir-fry	xào	*sòh*
Simmer	rim	*reem*
Roast	quay	*kway*
Mix	trộn	*choh·ụhn*
Sear	áp chảo	*aáp chỏw*

Places to eat

Restaurants	nhà hang	*nyaà haàng*
Eateries	quán	*kwaán*
Meals for office workers	cơm văn phòng	*ğerm vaang fòm*
Hot pot	lẩu	*law·ỏh*
Barbecue	nướng	*nuhr·érng*
Seafood eateries	quán ốc	*kwaán áwp*
Beer gardens	quán nhậu	*kwaán nyọh*

NUMBERS...

1	một	*mạwt*
2	hai	*hai*
3	ba	*baa*
4	bốn	*báwn*
5	năm	*nuhm*
6	sáu	*sóh*
7	bảy	*bảy*
8	tám	*dúhm*
9	chín	*jín*
10	mười	*muhr·eè*
20	hai mươi	*hai muhr·ee*
30	ba mươi	*ba muhr·ee*
40	bốn mươi	*báwn muhr·ee*
50	năm mươi	*nuhm muhr·ee*
60	sáu mươi	*sów muhr·ee*
70	bảy mươi	*bảy muhr·ee*
80	tám mươi	*daám muhr·ee*
90	chín mươi	*jín muhr·ee*
100	một trăm	*mạwt chuhm*
1000	một nghìn (N)	*mạwt ngyìn (N)*
	một ngàn (S)	*mọt ngaàn (S)*

finding a place to eat

Can you recommend a ...?	Bạn có thể giới thiệu một ... không?	*Baạn ğó tẻ zer·eé tee·oọ mạwt ...kawm*
bar	quán bar	*ğwaán baa*
café	quán càfê	*ğwaán ğaà·fe*
restaurant	nhà hàng	*nyaà haàng*
rice-and-noodle shop	quán ăn bình dân	*ğwaán uhn bìng zuhn*
Where would you go for (a) ...?	Những chỗ hay để ... ở đâu?	*Nyũhrng jãw hay đẻ ... ẻr đoh*
celebration	xem lễ hội	*sam lẽ họy*
cheap meal	ăn một bữa rẻ	*uhn mạwt bũhr·uh zã*
local specialities	đặc sản địa phương	*đụhk saản đee·ụh fuhr·erng*
I'd like to reserve a table for ...	Tôi muốn đặt bàn cho ...	*Doy moo·úhn đụht baàn jo ...*
(two) people	(hai) người	*(hai) nguhr·eè*
(eight) o'clock	vào lúc (tám) giờ	*vòw lúp (dúhm) zèr*
I'd like a/the ...	Xin cho tôi ...	*Sin jo doy ...*
children's menu	thực đơn cho trẻ em	*tụhrk đern jo chả am*
drink list	thực đơn đồ uống	*tụhrk đern đàw oo·úhng*
half portion	một nửa xuất	*mạwt nủhr·uh swúht*
menu (in English)	thực đơn (bằng tiếng Anh)	*tụhrk đern (bùhng dee·úhng aang)*
non-smoking section	bàn trong khu không hút thuốc	*baàn chom koo kawm hút too·úhk*
smoking section	bàn có hút thuốc	*baàn ğó hút too·úhk*
table for (five)	một bàn cho (năm) người	*mạwt baàn jo (nuhm) nguhr·eè*
Are you still serving food?	Bạn còn bán hàng không?	*Baạn ğòn baán haàng kawm*
How long is the wait?	Phải đợi bao nhiêu lâu?	*Faỉ đer·eẹ bow nyee·oo loh*

LISTEN FOR...

We're closed.	Đóng cửa rồi	*đóm ğủhr·uh zòy*
We're full.	Hết bàn rồi	*hét baàn zòy*
One moment.	Đợi một lát	*đer·eẹ mạwt laát*
Where would you like to sit?	Bạn muốn ngồi ở đâu?	*baạn moo·úhn ngòy ẻr đoh*
What can I get for you?	Bạn muốn ăn gì?	*baạn moo·úhn uhn zeè*
Here you go!	Thưa đây!	*tuhr·uh đay*
Enjoy your meal.	Chúc ngon miệng	*júp ngon mee·ụhng*

In a restaurant

What would you recommend?	Bạn có giới thiệu những món gì?	*baạn ğó zer·eé tee·oọ nyũhrng món zeè*
What's in that dish?	Có những gì ở trong cái đĩa kia?	*ğó nyũhrng zeè ẻr chom ğaí đeẽ·uh ğee·uh*
What's that called?	Món đó tên gì?	*món đó den zeè*
I'll have that.	Tôi chọn món đó.	*doy jọn món đó*
Does it take long to prepare?	Món đó có mất thời gian để làm không?	*món đó ğó múht ter·eè zaan đẻ laàm kawm*
Is it self-serve?	Có thể tự phục vụ không?	*ğó tẻ dụhr fụp voọ kawm*
Is there a cover charge?	Có phải mất tiền vào cửa?	*ğó faỉ múht dee·ùhn vòw ğủhr·uh*
Is service included in the bill?	Tiền boa có cộng vào hoá đơn?	*dee·ùhn bo·uh ğó ğạwm vòw hwaá đern*
Are these complimentary?	Cái này có khuyến mại không?	*ğaí này ğó kwee·úhn maị kawm*
Is there (a toilet)?	Có (phòng vệ sinh) không?	*ğó (fòm vẹ sinh) kawm*
I'd like it with ...	Tôi muốn ăn nó với ...	*doy moo·úhn uhn nó ver·eé ...*
I'd like it without ...	Tôi muốn ăn nó không có ...	*doy moo·úhn uhn nó kawm ğó ...*
butter	bơ	*ber*
chilli (sauce)	(tương) ớt	*(duhr·erng) ért*
garlic	tỏi	*dỏy*
ketchup	sốt cà chua	*sáwt ğaà joo·uh*
MSG	mì chính	*meè jíng*
nuts	hạt lạc	*haạt laạk*
oil	dầu ăn	*zòh uhn*
pepper	hạt tiêu	*haạt dee·oo*
salt	muối	*moo·eé*
tomato sauce	tương cà chua	*duhr·erng ğaà juhr·uh*
vinegar	dấm	*zúhm*
I'd like (a/the) ...	Tôi muốn ...	*doy moo·úhn ...*
local speciality	món đặc sản địa phương	*món đụhk saản đee·ụh fuhr·erng*
very good meal	một bữa ăn thật ngon	*mạwt bũhr·uh uhn tụht ngon*
menu	thực đơn	*baáng saan·wit*
that dish	món kia	*món ğee·uh*
Can I have (blanched bean sprouts), please?	Xin cho tôi (giá trụng)	*sin jo doy (zaá chụhrng)*

Meat & fish

beef	thịt bò	*tịt bò*
chicken	thịt gà	*tịt gaà*
crab	cua	*ğoo·uh*
eel	lươn	*luhr·ern*
fish	cá	*kaá*
frog	ếch	*ék*
goat	thịt dê	*tịt ze*
pork	thịt lợn (N) / heo (S)	*tịt lẹrn (N) / hay·o (S)*
prawns/shrimp	tôm	*dawm*
snail	ốc	*áwp*
squid	mực	*mụhrk*

Fruit & Veg

apple	táo (N) /bơm (S)	*dów (N) /berm (S)*
banana	chuối	*joo·eé*
carrot	cà rốt	*ğaà záwt*
coconut	dừa	*zuhr·ùh*
corn	ngô (N) /bắp (S)	*ngow (N) /búp (S)*
cucumber	dưa leo	*zuhr·uh lay·o*
eggplant/aubergine	cà tím	*ğaà dím*
grapes	nho	*nyo*
green beans	đậu xanh	*đọh saang*
lemon	chanh	*chaang*
lychee	vải	*vaỉ*
mandarin	quýt	*gweét*
mango	xoài	*swaì*
mushrooms	nấm	*núhm*
orange	cam	*ğaam*
papaya	đu đủ	*đoo đỏo*
pineapple	dứa	*zuhr·úh*
potato	khoai tây	*kwai day*
pumpkin	bí ngô	*beé ngaw*
strawberry	dâu	*zoh*
watermelon	dưa hấu	*zuhr·uh hóh*

Other

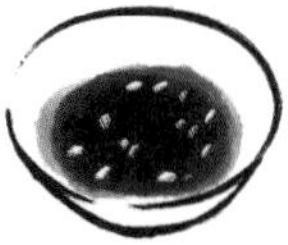

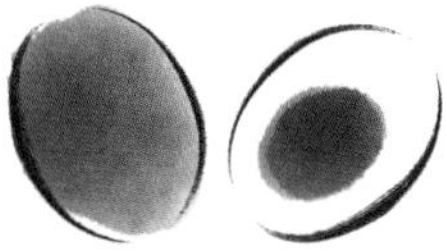

chilli sauce	tương ớt	*duhr·erng ért*
eggs	trứng	*chúhrng*
fish sauce	nước mắm	*nuhr·érk múhm*
flat rice noodles	phở	*fẻr*
fried rice	cơm rang	*ğerm zaang*
	thập cẩm (N)	*tụhp ğủhm*
	cơm chiên (S)	*ğerm jee·uhn*
rice	cơm	*ğerm*
salad	sa lát	*saa laát*
soup	canh	*ğaang*
steamed rice	cơm trắng	*ğerm chaáng*
ice	đá	*đaá*
pepper	hạt tiêu	*haạt dee·oo*
salt	muối	*moo·eé*
sugar	đường	*dur·èrng*
thin rice noodles	bún	*bún*
yellow egg noodles	mì	*meè*

At the table

Please bring (a/the) ...	Xin mang ...	*sin maang ...*
bill	hoá đơn	*hwaá đern*
cloth	khăn trải bàn	*kuhn chaỉ baàn*
(wine)glass	một ly (rượu)	*mạwt lee (zee·oọ)*
serviette	một khăn ăn	*mạwt kuhn uhn*
This is ...	Món này ...	*món này ...*
(too) cold	(quá) lạnh	*(ğwaá) laạng*
spicy	cay quá	*ğay ğwaá*
superb	tuyệt ngon	*dwee·ụht ngon*
I didn't order this.	Tôi không gọi món này	*doy kawm gọy món này*
There's a mistake in the bill.	Có sự nhầm lẫn trên hoá đơn	*ğó sụhr nyùhm lữhn chen hwaá đern*

Talking food

I love this dish!	Món này ngon thế!	*món này ngon té*
I love the local cuisine.	Tôi rất thích những món ăn ở đây	*doy zúht tík nhũhrng món uhn ẻr đay*
That was delicious!	Ngon tuyệt!	*ngon dwee·ụht*
My compliments to the chef.	Đầu bếp thật tài ba	*đòh bép tụht daì baa*
I'm full.	Tôi no rồi	*doy no zòy*

Preferences and Allergies

I'm a vegetarian.	Tôi ăn chay	*doy uhn jay*
I'm a vegan.	Tôi ăn chay thuần	*doy uhn jay thoo·ùhn*
I'm allergic to (shrimp).	Tôi bị dị ứng với (tôm)	*doy beẹ zeẹ úhrng ver·eé (dawm)*
Does this food contain ...?	Món này có chứa ...?	*Máwn này ğó chuhr·úh ...?*
grains	ngũ gốc	*ngoo ğáwp*
wheat	lúa mì	*loó·uh meè*
wheat flour	bột mì	*bạwt meè*
barley	lúa mạch	*loó·uh mạhk*
rye	lúa mạch đen	*loó·uh mạhk den*
oats	yến mạch	*ee·én mạhk*
soy sauce	xì dầu	*seè zòh*
milk	sữa	*sũhr·uh*
condensed milk	sữa đặc	*sũhr·uh dạwk*
soy bean	đậu nành	*dọh naàng*
eggs	trứng	*chúhrng*
nuts/seeds	hạt	*haạt*

Non-alcoholic drinks

Boiled water	nước sôi	
Hot water	nước nóng	*nuhr·érk soy*
Orange juice	nước cam	*nuhr·érk nóm*
Soft drink	nước ngọt	*nuhr·érk ğaam*
Sparkling mineral water	nước sô-đa	*nuhr·érk ngọk*
Still mineral water	nước suối	*nuhr·érk saw·đaa*
		nuhr·érk soo·eé
(Cup of) coffee ...	(một cốc) cà phê ...	
(Cup of) tea ...	(một cốc) trà ...	*(mạwt ğáwp) ğaà fe ...*
with milk	có sữa	*(mạwt ğáwp) chaà ...*
without milk	không sữa	*ğó sũhr·uh*
with sugar	có đường	*kawm sũhr·uh*
without sugar	không có đường	*ğó đuhr·èrng*
		kawm ğó đuhr·èrng

COFFEE

*Vietnamese coffee is a notoriously strong brew and, mixed with the high-sugar hit from a whack of condensed milk, a caffeine buzz is inevitable. Don't bother asking for it strong (*mạnh *maạng). You can try asking for it weak (*nhẹ *nyạ), but it's likely to get you bouncing all the same.*

Coffee...	cà phê...	*ğaà fe...*
black	đen	*đan*
iced black	đá	*đaá*
iced white	sữa đá	*sũhr·uh đaá*
strong	loại mạnh	*lwaị maạng*
white	sữa	*sũhr·uh*

Alcoholic drinks

Brandy	rượu brandi	*zee·oọ braan·đee*
Champagne	rượu sâm banh	*zee·oọ suhm baang*
Cocktail	côctai	*ğawk·tai*
A shot of ...	một ngụm rượu ...	*mạwt ngụm zee·oọ ...*
gin	gin	*jin*
rum	rom	*zom*
tequila	têquila	*te·kee·laa*
vodka	vốtka	*váwt·ğaa*
whisky	uytky	*wit·ğee*
A bottle/glass of ... wine	một chai/cốc rượu vang ...	*mạwt jai/ğáwp zee·oọ vaang ...*
dessert	tráng miệng	*chaáng mee·ụhng*
red	đỏ	*đỏ*
sparkling	có ga	*ğó gaa*
white	trắng	*chaáng*
A ... of beer	một ... bia	*mạwt ... bi·uh*
glass	cốc (N) /ly (S)	*ğáwp (N) /lee (S)*
jug	bình	*bìng*
large bottle	chai to	*jai do*
small bottle	chai nhỏ	*jai nyỏ*

In the bar

Cheers!	Chúc sức khoẻ!	*júp súhrk kwả*
Excuse me!	Xin lỗi!	*sin lõy*
I'm next.	Đã đến lượt của tôi	*đaã đén luhr·ẹrt ğoỏ·uh doy*
I'll have ...	Cho tôi ...	*jo doy ...*
Same again, please.	Cho một cái nữa	*jo mạwt ğaí nũhr·uh*
No ice, thanks.	Đừng cho đá vào	*đùhrng jo đaá vòw*
I'll buy you a drink.	Cho tôi mua một ly rượu cho bạn	*jo doy moo·uh mạwt lee zee·oọ jo baạn*
What would you like?	Bạn thích uống gì?	*baạn tík oo·úhng zeè*
I don't drink alcohol.	Tôi không biết uống rượu	*doy kawm bee·úht oo·úhng zee·oọ*
It's my round.	Đến lượt của tôi, tôi phải trả	*đén luhr·ẹrt ğoỏ·uh doy doy faỉ chaả*

LOCAL DRINKS

draught beer	bia tươi (N) / hơi (S)	*bee·uh duhr·ee (N)/ her·ee (S)*
coconut water	nước dừa	*nuhr·érk zuhr·ùh*
sugar-cane juice	nước mía	*nuhr·érk mee·úh*
rice wine	rượu nếp	*zee·oọ nép*

How much is that?	Cái đó bao nhiêu?	*ğaí đó bow nyee·oo*
Do you serve meals here?	Có phục vụ đồ ăn ở đây không?	*ğó fụp voọ đàw uhn ẻr đay kawm*
I'm drunk.	Tôi say rồi	*doy say zòy*

INDEX

Published in May 2021 by Lonely Planet
Global Limited CRN 554153
www.lonelyplanet.com
ISBN 978 18386 9050 2

10 9 8 7 6 5 4 3 2 1
Printed in Malaysia

Written by: Barbara Adam and James Pham
Managing Director, Publishing: Piers Pickard
Associate Publisher: Robin Barton
Editors: Jessica Cole, Nora Rawn, Polly Thomas, Clifton Wilkinson
Art Direction: Daniel Di Paolo
Layout Designer: Jo Dovey
Cover illustration: © Muti, Folio Art
Spot Illustrations: Louise Sheeren, Tina García, Daniel Di Paolo
Print Production: Nigel Longuet

Lonely Planet offices
USA
230 Franklin Road, Building 2B, Franklin, TN 37064
T: 615-988-9713

IRELAND
Digital Depot, Roe Lane (off Thomas St),
Digital Hub, Dublin 8, D08 TCV4

STAY IN TOUCH lonelyplanet.com/contact